Girls Like Me

Girls Like Me

Illustrated by:
Aurélia Durand, Sinem Erkas,
Tinuke Fagborun, Caribay Marquina,
Frieda Ruh, Ana Strumpf,
Libby VanderPloeg, and Yifan Wu

Contents

6	Welcome
8	A Note From the Editors

10 AFRICA

12	**ANGOLA**
14	Ana
16	**MOROCCO**
18	Khadija
20	**SOUTH AFRICA**
22	Mia
24	**TANZANIA**
26	Elizabeth
28	Gloria

30 ASIA

32	**BANGLADESH**
34	Sumaiya
36	Mim
38	**CAMBODIA**
40	Linka
42	Dalin
44	**CHINA**
46	Tingxi
48	Jingyi
50	Yihuan Cao
52	Shi Guiting
54	**INDIA**
56	Siya
58	Aadya
60	**JAPAN**
62	Meisa
64	**KAZAKHSTAN**
66	Leisan
68	**LAOS**
70	Chitsavanh
72	**MALAYSIA**
74	Zi Zhi
76	**NEPAL**
78	Gurans
80	Subina
82	**SINGAPORE**
84	Arya
86	**SOUTH KOREA**
88	Bitna
90	**SRI LANKA**
92	Binuli

94 EUROPE

96	**DENMARK**
98	Eva
100	**FINLAND**
102	Stella
104	**FRANCE**
106	Rita
108	**GERMANY**
110	Lisa
112	Thea
114	**GREECE**
116	Myrsini
118	**IRELAND**
120	Naomi
122	**ITALY**
124	Sofia

Gurans p.78

Thea p.112

126	**THE NETHERLANDS**
128	Liv
130	Maeve

| 132 | **PORTUGAL** |
| 134 | Nathalie |

| 136 | **SLOVAKIA** |
| 138 | Anna |

140	**SPAIN**
142	Helena
144	Alba
146	Martina

| 148 | **SWEDEN** |
| 150 | Clara |

| 152 | **SWITZERLAND** |
| 154 | Alice |

| 156 | **TÜRKIYE** |
| 158 | Vera |

160	**UNITED KINGDOM**
162	Avalon
164	Safaa
166	Millie
168	Sidney
170	René & Matilda
172	Leela

| 174 | **NORTH AMERICA** |

176	**CANADA**
178	Maya
180	Aiva

182	**THE CARIBBEAN**
184	Faith
186	Aerin

188	**UNITED STATES**
190	Ruhee
192	Beatriz
194	Charlotte
196	Colette
198	Isabella
200	Madeline
202	Rachael

| 204 | **SOUTH AMERICA** |

| 206 | **ARGENTINA** |
| 208 | Ema |

| 210 | **BRAZIL** |
| 212 | Amora |

| 214 | **COLOMBIA** |
| 216 | Salomé |

| 218 | **ECUADOR** |
| 220 | Nicole |

| 222 | **PERU** |
| 224 | Camila |

| 226 | **OCEANIA** |

228	**AUSTRALIA**
230	Willow
232	Clementine

| 234 | **NEW ZEALAND** |
| 236 | Molly |

238	**WHEN PEOPLE MOVE**
240	Gauri
242	Jo & Elsa
244	Eleanor
246	Francesca

248	Let's Say "Hello"
250	How We Made This Book
252	About Rebel Girls
254	Credits
255	Meet the Illustrators

Helena p.142

Maya p.178

Camila p.224

Molly p.236

Francesca p.246

Welcome

Have you ever wondered what it's like to grow up somewhere else?

What does Tingxi from China eat for breakfast? How does Nathalie from Portugal celebrate her birthday? What does Ana from Angola do for fun? What does Chitsavanh from Laos wear to school?

We talked to Rebel Girls on all six inhabited continents of the world about their lives: their daily routines, their homes, their passions, their hopes, their inspirations, and what it's really like to live in their countries.

We invite you to travel through the pages of this book and meet girls around the world to learn how they live their lives and dream their dreams. How does a country and its culture shape the people who live there? What do we all have in common and what makes us unique? Let's find out!

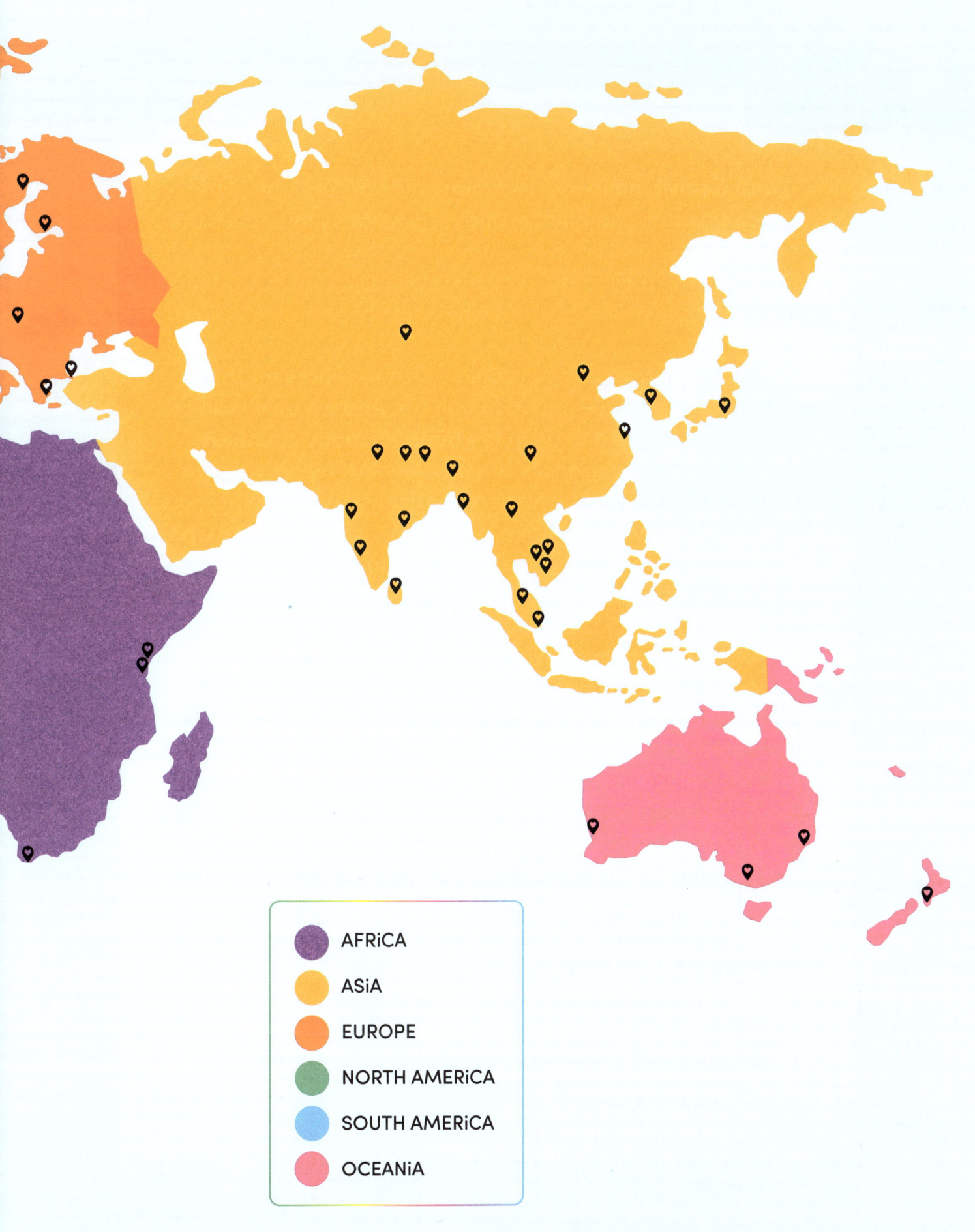

A Note From the Editors

What a privilege to meet so many girls around the world, whose passions, ambitions, and inspirations jumped off the page of their applications. Getting to know a generation of girls who ask questions – who are curious about how others live, what they believe in, and why – has been truly inspiring.

Remember, no one girl could begin to represent the experience of a whole nation or culture. And we only featured girls who applied to be in the book, so many countries, cultures, and experiences are missing. But by providing a snapshot of girls' lives across six continents, we hope to show just how much you can have in common with someone who looks and sounds very unlike you, to spotlight our connectedness as well as all our wonderful differences.

Girlhood is a unique experience that comes with its challenges. Some girls spoke meaningfully about health difficulties, loneliness, friendship troubles, parents who have separated, pets who have died, or their struggle to fit in and find their place in the world. Many of our Rebel Girls talked about the importance of family, kindness, and support. If you are having a tough time, we hope that you will find comfort in the pages of this book, and know that you are not alone.

Wherever you are from, we hope you read this book and see that girls with passion and curiosity are powerful, and are even more powerful together.

We can't wait to see what you Rebel Girls accomplish.

AFRiCA

North Atlantic Ocean

Angola

Running along the west coast of southern Africa, Angola has a cool mix of beaches, grassy savannahs, humid rainforests, and dry deserts. The capital, Luanda, is a lively city on the ocean, where skyscrapers rise above the crashing waves. It has one of the world's youngest populations, with almost 65 per cent of Angolans under the age of 25. There are exciting opportunities in green energy ahead for Angola, as the country has pledged to embrace more renewable energy projects like solar power plants.

Language, Music, and Dance

Forty-seven different languages are spoken across Angola. Two of these are Umbundu and Kimbundu. Music is a huge part of national identity, as is dance, and different sounds and moves have their origins in different parts of the country. *Ndimbu* is a traditional warrior dance to an energetic beat, and *Semba*, a more modern style, featured in the viral Jerusalema Dance Challenge of 2020.

The Moon on Earth

Just outside Angola's capital, Luanda, there is a place with beauty that's otherworldly. It is called Miradouro da Lua, which means "Viewpoint of the Moon". This amazing geological hotspot has tall, twisty cliffs made of red, orange, and yellow rock shaped by wind and rain over millions of years. When the sun sets, the whole landscape glows like fire.

A Turbulent History

From the end of the 1300s, the land now known as Angola was ruled by powerful kingdoms. The Black Rocks at Pungo Andongo still remain at the heart of what used to be the Kingdom of Ndongo. These breathtaking stones were considered sacred. Portuguese colonizers first arrived in the 1400s, and in 1671, they took control of the country in order to exploit its resources. Angola gained its independence from Portugal many centuries later, in 1975, but due to the legacies of colonialism, a long civil war soon broke out, lasting 27 years. The country is now rebuilding and growing.

FAST FACTS

Official Name: Republic of Angola

Capital: Luanda

Location: Southern Africa

Official Language: Portuguese

Currency: Angolan Kwanza

Border Countries: Democratic Republic of the Congo, Namibia, Republic of the Congo, Zambia

Population: 37.89 million

Area: 1.247 million km²

Natural Wonders

Kissama National Park in northwestern Angola is home to elephants, zebras, and giant sable antelopes – the country's national animal, which was once considered extinct until it was rediscovered here in 2005. Angola's most impressive natural wonder lies 400 kilometres inland, in Malanje Province. The majestic Kalandula Falls is one of the world's largest waterfalls at 105 metres high and 400 metres wide, where water thunders down cliffs as high as a 25-storey building!

KALANDULA FALLS

LUANDA

Did you know? The Namib boasts some of the world's tallest sand dunes, reaching up to 305 metres in height.

Desert Sands

In the far south of Angola, golden sand dunes stretch for miles through one of the oldest deserts in the world: the Namib. It is a harsh environment, yet some of the world's oldest plants survive here. The amazing *Welwitschia mirabilis* is sometimes referred to as a living fossil; some specimens are more than 1,000 years old! During its life, each plant produces only two long leaves. They split into many segments as a result of being whipped by the high desert winds.

We Have Lift Off!

Angola is reaching for the stars with its National Space Programme, which has its HQ in Luanda. Its first satellites were launched into space in 2017 and 2022, to provide TV, internet, and radio capabilities to Angola and beyond. Comic books about space technology were given to children to inspire Angola's space scientists of the future.

REBEL GiRLS OF ANGOLA

Queen Nzinga (b. 1582) ruled the Mbundu kingdoms of Ndongo and Matamba during the 1600s. She was a skilful politician, who worked to protect her people against colonialism.

Lília da Fonseca (b. 1906) was a Portuguese and Angolan journalist and writer, born in the city of Benguela. She was a feminist and was the first woman to run for legislative office, in 1957.

Ana

My nickname is Lelo

Age: 12

My home:
I live with my mom, dad, and sister. We all speak Portuguese. I share a bedroom with my sister. It is painted green and white. My favourite thing in it is a chest that I keep my treasures in. I help around the house by tidying, helping in the kitchen, and washing clothes. We don't have any pets.

My city:
I like my city, Luanda, because it has very friendly people. It is the capital of Angola, and is the most populated Portuguese-speaking capital city in the world. It is right on the beach, with skyscrapers and palm trees. It's a big and beautiful city with many job opportunities, but I would like the security, sanitation, hygiene, and health services to improve.

My country is famous for its beautiful beaches. I love to go to the beach with my friends. We hang out, play, and talk about life and school. The Mussulo peninsula is 10 minutes from Luanda by boat; the water there is calm, and you can spend the day relaxing on the sand.

School starts at 7am and finishes at 12:35pm. We have lessons in maths, physics, chemistry, history, Portuguese language, and more. I enjoy learning new things and being at school. I'm proud of the fact that I've never failed a grade and that I'm good at maths. My favourite subjects are maths, Portuguese language, English, and physics.

We travel everywhere in taxis called *candongueiros*. They are 12–15 seater vans, which are the most common form of transport in Luanda. They can be lively and fun! *Kuduro* is a special type of music that started here in Luanda. It spread when lots of kuduro musicians gave CDs to the taxi drivers so their music could be heard by everybody in the city!

My mom and aunt are such inspiring women. I love spending time with them. I look forward to shopping with my mom and going to church with her. I enjoy reading very much. I read the Bible, poetry, and stories, or I go on my phone. For sports, I like athletics, basketball, and football.

Carnival is the biggest celebration of the year here. It happens just before Lent. For three days, Luanda's streets fill with incredible costumes, music, and dancing. We are right across the Atlantic from Brazil, another former Portuguese colony, and our Carnival is similar to theirs. But our costumes show off beautiful African prints and braids, often featuring the colours of the Angolan flag: red, yellow, and black.

REBEL GIRL SUPERPOWER: I WORK HARD AT SCHOOL

Port Importance

Morocco is important in global trade, with a 3,500-kilometre coastline that runs along both the Mediterranean and Atlantic seas. The port city of Tangier is only 27 kilometres from the southern tip of Spain and, as the gateway between Africa and Europe, has been a desirable trade route since ancient times. The development of the huge new Tangier-Med port is helping to grow Morocco's economy.

Morocco

Morocco hugs the northwest corner of Africa. The vast Sahara Desert separates its milder coast from the Atlas Mountains, where the Amazigh people have lived for centuries. Morocco draws more tourists than any other country in Africa – they come to explore bustling *souks* (markets) and medieval city *medinas* (centres). Morocco is home to nearly 38 million Muslim people, 99 per cent of the population. Architectural gems include a number of famous mosques, from the 1000-year-old Ben Youssef to the 20th-century Hassan II.

Desert Dunes

The Sahara, the world's largest hot desert, covers much of southern Morocco. With giant sand dunes reaching up to 150 metres tall, it looks like a sea of golden waves. Hardy animals like the fennec fox, and hopping rodents called jerboa thrive in the arid environment. At night, the stars put on a show in the clear, dark skies above. With a lack of light pollution in the Sahara, celestial wonders like the Milky Way can be seen by stargazers.

FAST FACTS

Official Name: Kingdom of Morocco

Capital: Rabat

Location: Northwest Africa, Maghreb

Official Language: Arabic, Tamazight

Currency: Moroccan Dirham

Border Countries: Algeria, Western Sahara (disputed territory)

Population: 38 million

Area: 446,550 km²

Tea and Tagine

Moroccan dishes typically blend bold flavours like spices, fruits, and meats together. Tagine is a slow-cooked stew made in a special (often beautifully painted) pot, usually served with fluffy couscous. Couscous is a mainstay of the Moroccan diet and is enjoyed at home and during celebrations. Refreshing mint tea, sweetened with sugar, is served as a symbol of hospitality when visiting someone's home or shop.

Inspired Artists

Moroccan art is a wonder of intricate mosaic tilework (*zellige*), calligraphy, textiles, and pottery, with a strong emphasis on geometric patterns and bright colours. Moroccan artist Amina Agueznay won the prestigious Norval Sovereign African Art prize in 2024 with her woven piece titled "Portal #1". She was inspired by the geometric patterns and symbols she saw painted on rural village doors.

ATLAS MOUNTAINS

Atlas Mountains

The vast ranges of the Atlas Mountains stretch for more than 2,000 kilometres across three countries, starting in the southwest of Morocco. The highest peak is Morocco's Mount Toubkal, at a lofty 4,164 metres. Hikers in the Atlas Mountains might see waterfalls flowing through deep valleys, cedar forests, and snowy peaks, as well as Amazigh village settlements. And, if they're very lucky they might even catch sight of the rare and elusive Barbary leopard.

Red and Blue Cities

In many Moroccan cities, lots of the buildings are similar colours. Marrakesh is known as the "Red City" for its buildings constructed with beaten clay and sandstone. Chefchaouen, high in the mountains, is known as the "Blue City" for its turquoise and cobalt buildings. Casablanca, by the Atlantic Ocean, dates back to 15 BCE, but has embraced modern architecture, with tall, impressive buildings like the Hassan II Mosque. Fez is considered Morocco's cultural and religious capital.

Did you know? The Hassan II Mosque is the second-largest functioning mosque in the whole of Africa.

Blue City

REBEL GIRLS OF MOROCCO

Pokimane (b. 1996) is one of the most viewed Twitch streamers online, where she plays video games like *Fortnite* and *League of Legends* for audiences of millions around the world.

Merieme Chadid (b. 1969), a pioneering astronomer and astrophysicist, helped to build the VLT observatory in Chile. In 2005, she became the first Moroccan woman to set foot in Antarctica.

Khadija

I want to work with computers

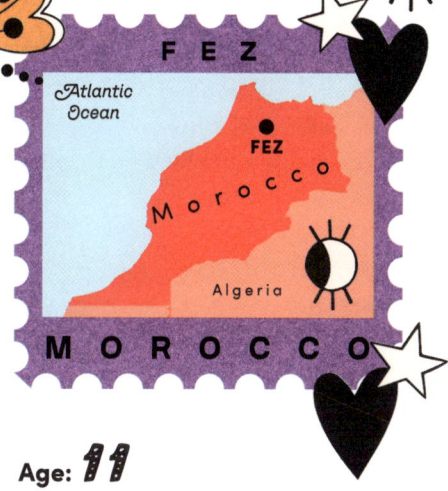

We speak Arabic, French, and English at school. The language we speak depends on the subject that we're learning at the time. I love English class because it allows me to discover a whole new culture.

I like travelling on the school bus, because I get to have conversations with friends from different grades. Sometimes school can be boring, but most of the time it is interesting because I get to learn new things.

I'm in the coding club at school, and I love to draw. I want to be an informatics engineer or a computer scientist when I am older.

There are so many traditional Moroccan dishes, you could eat a different one every day of the week! On Fridays, my family eats Moroccan couscous. I really love chicken *bastilla*, which is a type of pie that's made across the Maghreb (Northwest Africa). You make it with chicken, eggs, toasted almonds, and warm spices like cinnamon, all cased in crispy filo pastry. I love the mix of sweet and salty flavours.

I enjoy weddings because everyone is happy. It's wonderful to share great memories and see the bride being made to feel special. I wear my Moroccan caftan to weddings and special events. It's my favourite outfit.

I love my four sisters. Two of them have left home now, and I'm happiest when we get to see them. I begged one of my sisters to share a room with me! Our room is covered in butterflies. We love butterflies because even though they only live a short life, their beauty stays in your mind for a lifetime.

Age: 11

My home:
I live with my mom, my dad, and two of my four sisters, in a house in the city. My other two sisters have left home: one lives in our capital city, Rabat, and the other lives in Germany. My third sister, Aya, is living with us while she studies medicine. We used to have a pet cat, but we lost him; it was the worst experience.

My city:
I live in Fez, which is northwest of the Atlas Mountains in Morocco. At the weekend we often drive in our car to the nearby mountains. Fez is one of the oldest cities in Morocco and has many historic sites, including the first university in the world! We have two old medina quarters, one of which is almost preserved exactly as it was when it was a medieval city, and a more modern area, too.

South Africa

Welcome to the "Rainbow Nation", nestled right at Africa's tip. It is a country with a kaleidoscope of cultures, ethnicities, and languages – and a history that shows how people can come together after segregation. South Africa's land and marine wildlife are also very diverse, from aardvarks and antelopes to sharks, dolphins, and penguins. Mineral-rich South Africa's thriving cities, including Johannesburg and Cape Town, house over two-thirds of the country's population.

Peaks and Plains

The Drakensberg Mountains (Dragon's Mountains) rise high, with rocky cliffs and waterfalls, but the Karoo semi-desert is arid. Much of South Africa is covered with dry grasslands, called *highveld*, and plains sparsely covered with trees, called *bushveld*. The Garden Route is a 300-kilometre stretch of coast, named after its greenery, forests, rivers, and flowers. Further east, the Wild Coast is known for rugged cliffs and quiet beaches.

Did you know?
South Africa is the only country where the Atlantic and Indian Oceans meet.

FAST FACTS

Official Name: Republic of South Africa

Capitals: Bloemfontein (judicial), Cape Town (legislative), Pretoria (administrative)

Currency: Rand

Population: 64 million

Area: 1.219 million km²

Border Countries: Botswana, Eswatini, Lesotho, Mozambique, Namibia, Zimbabwe

Official Languages: Afrikaans, English, Ndebele, Xhosa, Zulu, Sepedi, Sesotho, Setswana, siSwati, Tshivenda, Xitsonga

First Fossils

Important fossils and cave paintings first discovered within the Sterkfontein Caves in northern South Africa have helped us to understand human evolution. Buried deep under the cool earth near Johannesburg, archaeologists found "Mrs Ples", the skull of a distant pre-human relative. The area is known as the "Cradle of Humankind" as it is the birthplace of some of the earliest extinct relatives of modern humans.

Rainbow Nation

A group of white South Africans called Afrikaners ruled under the apartheid system of racial segregation until 1994. When Nelson Mandela became the first elected Black president, Archbishop Desmond Tutu coined the nickname "Rainbow Nation" to describe South Africa in its new era of unity. There is much work still to be done, but now the country's many cultures have a voice. The National Anthem has verses in Xhosa, Zulu, Sesotho, Afrikaans, and English – just some of its 11 official languages. The national flower, the beautiful King Protea, is a resilient species that regrows after wildfires, symbolizing the hope and strength of a nation reborn.

The Sardine Run

One of nature's most spectacular events happens off South Africa's east coast between May and July each year. Millions of sardines migrate north from their home off the southern coast, creating a truly massive school that attracts sharks, dolphins, whales, and diving birds. Marine biologists and hobbyist divers travel from all over the world to witness this incredible gathering of species, one of the largest migrations of organisms on the planet.

THE 2025 SPRiNGBOKS

Biological Hotspot

At least 5,000 species of plant can be found here and nowhere else in the world! The Cape Floral Region covers 13 protected areas of exceptional plants and wildlife, including Cape Town's Table Mountain National Park, with its flat-top mountain and the famous penguins of Boulders Beach. Kruger National Park is one of the largest game reserves in Africa, where thundering rhinos mingle with prickly porcupines.

Springbok Success

South Africa's greatest sporting obsession is the Springboks – the nickname for the nation's rugby teams. The men's team are rugby GOATs, winning a record four World Cups, and now the women's team are making their own bold moves on the world stage. In 2025, the Boks women qualified for their first ever World Cup quarter finals, inspiring all South African girls who dream of wearing the green and gold national kit.

REBEL GIRLS OF SOUTH AFRICA

The **Black Mambas** are the world's first all-female anti-poaching unit. These dedicated women walk 20 kilometres every day, patrolling South Africa's Greater Kruger National Park to protect the rhino population.

Zenzile Miriam Makeba or Mama Africa (b. 1932) was born in Johannesburg. As a South African singer and civil rights activist, she is known for becoming one of the first African artists to globally popularize African music.

Mia

I love being homeschooled

**CAPE TOWN
SOUTH AFRICA**

Age: 11

My home:
I live with my parents and my older brother, Josh (13). We live in a bungalow on a mountain. My backyard is fairly big and sloped. What's really unique is that we can see both the Indian and the Atlantic Oceans from our deck! I have my own bedroom. It is very bright and colourful.

My city:
I live in Fish Hoek, a coastal suburb of Cape Town. Fish Hoek is a beautiful place and a popular tourist attraction. Our beach is long, with rock pools to explore, and the bay is sheltered so it is good for swimming and boogie boarding. Cape Town is South Africa's oldest city and the seat of the Parliament of South Africa. It sits beneath Table Mountain.

"Homeschooling teaches you that anything can be a learning opportunity. There is more than one way of learning."

The pandemic made us realize we enjoyed doing school differently. I usually stay at home for my lessons, but every so often we go to the beach or on a hike as schoolwork. My mom mainly sets my subjects. I get to choose a few of the less important ones. My favourite subject this year is learning about history through fashion.

When I see my friends, we mostly have sleepovers. Being homeschooled, I don't see them at school, but that's OK! We also see each other at church on Sundays and have a book club every second Sunday. I love reading and am obsessed with murder mysteries.

I have a rare bone condition, called Chronic Recurrent Multifocal Osteomyelitis (CRMO), which means that my body attacks my bones. CRMO is not something many people have heard of, and it can be really hard when my condition flares up. I have to walk on crutches when the pain in my legs is too much. I'm proud to show that CRMO doesn't make me a weak person. It takes a lot of resilience to manage a chronic illness.

I take extracurricular classes. We call them extra murals here. I do ballet, French, singing, drama, piano, and art. For the longest time I wanted to be a singer, but I'm starting to enjoy my ballet more and more so I'd like to be either a singer or a dancer when I'm older. I love Taylor Swift, and I'm proud of getting 96 per cent at a singing *eisteddfod*, which is a competitive performing arts event where singers of different ages and skill levels perform for judges.

My dog's name is Gandalf. He was named by his rescue shelter, but it's appropriate because I love *The Lord of the Rings*! There were fires two years ago, and he was found in a bad state. My cat is called Ginger Star, named by a little me.

Tanzania

Where can you see lions, giraffes, and elephants in the wild, climb Africa's tallest mountain, *and* dip your toes in the Indian Ocean? Tanzania, the largest country in East Africa! Though its capital Dodoma and most populous city Dar es Salaam are busy and thriving urban centres, the vast majority of Tanzania's population lives in rural communities. Tanzania also includes the islands of Zanzibar, Mafia, and Pemba, that are located to the east of the mainland.

Mongooses mostly eat insects like termites, which they dig out of mounds with their sharp claws!

Food and Drink

Many people in Tanzania are farmers and fishers. Common dishes include *ugali* (a type of cornmeal porridge), *sambusa* (fried pastries with meat or vegetables), and fresh fish from the sea or lakes. The huge Lake Tanganyika is an important source of food for many people. Delicious fruits like mangoes, pineapples, and bananas grow readily, while coffee plants provide beans to be enjoyed locally or sold to other countries.

Education and Inspiration

There are many projects in Tanzania set up by government and international organizations to empower and inspire girls and women through education. For example, a dormitory next to Lagosa Secondary School in the rural west provides a safe space for 80 girls to eat and sleep on school premises, maximizing their time for study but also for building community with their friends. The dormitory was built by the Tuungane Project, a joint partnership between The Nature Conservancy and Pathfinder International. The KINARA mentoring programme was co-developed by young Tanzanian women to improve the representation of women in top positions across the country. It supports young women and girls learning leadership skills, so that they can thrive in their careers and become leaders of the future. Kinara means "beacon" in Swahili.

FAST FACTS

Official Name: United Republic of Tanzania

Capital: Dodoma

Location: East Africa

Official Languages: Swahili, English

Currency: Tanzanian Shilling

Border countries: Burundi, Democratic Republic of the Congo, Kenya, Malawi, Mozambique, Rwanda, Uganda, Zambia

Population: 68.56 million

Area: 947,300 km²

Majestic Mountain

Mount Kilimanjaro is the highest mountain in the whole of Africa! It stands at 5,895 metres tall. People from all over the world travel to Tanzania to climb it. It was once an active volcano and has three volcanic cones: Kibo, Mawenzi, and Shira. It is known for its snow-capped top, even though Tanzania's climate is mostly warm.

Did you know? A group of zebras is called a "dazzle", and a group of hyenas is called a "cackle"!

Islands and the Coast

Zanzibar is a group of islands found off the coast in the Indian Ocean, and home to around 1.8 million people. Despite being part of the United Republic of Tanzania, Zanzibar has its own president and holds elections every five years. Zanzibari schoolchildren can take part in education programmes about protecting the precious coral reefs, inspiring the next generation of local ocean guardians.

ZANZIBAR

Maasai Women Making Change

The MWEDO Collective was set up by three Maasai women to create an empowering network for other Maasai women. MWEDO has a school, a health facility, and 500 weekly support groups where 10,000 women can come together to start businesses and learn about their legal rights to own land.

The Big Five

National parks cover more than a third of Tanzania, making it a popular destination for nature tourism. Incredible animals like giraffes, zebras, wildebeest, and cheetahs can be seen on the vast plains of the Serengeti, whose name comes from a Maasai word meaning "the place where the land runs on forever". The Ngorongoro Crater is another place to spot the "Big Five": lions, elephants, leopards, buffalo, and rhinos!

REBEL GIRLS OF TANZANIA

World-renowned paediatrician **Esther Mwaikambo** (b. 1940) grew up in the foothills of Mount Kilimanjaro and worked hard to become the first woman doctor in Tanzania, in 1969.

Performing artist and youth activist **Vanessa Mdee** (b. 1988) was the first ever Tanzanian presenter on MTV. In 2013 she was added to the Dar es Salaam hub of the World Economic Forum.

Elizabeth

My friends call me Eliza

I get to school in a *DalaDala* – a type of converted truck that is our main form of public transport. Classes start at 6:30am with a morning speed test, and run until 5pm. When I get home, I do my chores, read school library books with my siblings, and sit down for dinner at about 9pm.

I enjoy reading with my friends, especially books that encourage girls to have self-confidence and courage. Through books, we share ideas on conserving the environment, career aspirations, and building positive mindsets. When we're not reading we love skipping!

I love wearing dresses in African prints and fabrics. Representing our African culture is important to me. *Kitenge* is a colourful, wax-printed fabric that originated in East Africa and is used for clothes and home decor.

Studying science fuels my curiosity – about the world around me, and about the amazing human body. Exploring STEM subjects helps me to improve my problem-solving skills and supports my career goal of becoming a doctor.

I enjoy our end-of-year celebration. All our relatives meet at our *boma* (a local group of houses). We eat meat with a stew made of plantain and beans called *kiburu*. We dance a traditional dance called *iringi* while drinking *mbege* – a drink made from cooked, ripe bananas that are left to ferment for three days, then mixed with water and cooked malt.

I'm proud that I'm a confident girl, who believes that she is capable of doing things that most people think only boys can do. I want to encourage my fellow girls, and show them that we can pursue traditionally masculine careers such as engineering or medicine. We can take care of our families and ensure that children receive a good education.

"Studying science helps me to understand why different things happen."

Age: 12

My home:
I live with my mother, my brother, Goodluck (9), and my sister, Veronica (4). My father died when I was younger. Our house is gated and we have a garden where we grow some of our food. We have banana plants, a guava tree, and a swing. I share a room with my siblings; it is decorated with a reading timetable, a wardrobe, and shoes. We have a dog, called Dog! He protects our home.

My city:
I live in Dar es Salaam. It's a busy city with a large population. It has a train station and a main bus terminal that serves the countryside as well as neighbouring countries like Zambia, Rwanda, Burundi, and Democratic Republic of the Congo.

Gloria

I take care of anything I can

My nickname is Mama Kay, after the Nigerian actress and comedian Oby Kechere. She goes by Ms Koi Koi (or Mama Kay in Nigerian Pidgin). My mother says I used to be as funny as her when I was little, and her work outside of acting to promote the importance of vaccinations is so inspiring.

I am passionate about learning English. I want to become a tour guide when I'm older so it's really important. I love travelling, and above all, it will give me the chance to spend time in nature. I'm always happiest when I'm outside. I love watching football, too. Young Africans Sports Club is my favourite team in Tanzania.

My friends and I like chatting about our lives. We talk about school subjects, fun activities we're looking forward to like holiday plans, what makes us happy, and what makes us sad. Sometimes we sit around and discuss annoying boys in our class! I'm proud that I'm a shoulder to cry on when my friends are struggling with various issues in their lives; I try to support them however I can.

I walk to school each day, but I travel by car or motorbike for long-distance journeys. When I'm at home, I help out by washing dishes, taking care of our chickens, helping my grandmother to take her medicine, and mopping the floor. I help my aunt to prepare dinner most nights. We often eat *ugali*, a sort of stiff porridge, with vegetables and fish, but rice with beans is my favourite meal.

Age: 12

My home:
I live with my aunt, my sister, Mariam (16), and our grandmother. Mariam and I share a room. We don't have any decorations, but I love our comfy bed. I speak Swahili with my family and at school.

My town:
I live in a town called Muheza, near the northeast coast of Tanzania. It is famous for being one of the leading producers of coconuts, oranges, and spices in the country. More than 80 per cent of Tanzania's oranges are grown here in Muheza.

"I'm inspired by Tulia Ackson, Speaker of the National Assembly. She is confident and wise."

I love taking care of all living things, nurturing them and helping them to grow and flourish. Animals, plants, flowers – I love them all! We only have chickens at home, because some of my family members don't like cats and dogs, but I do, especially dogs.

Bangladesh

Welcome to one of the world's most densely populated countries. This is especially true in its bustling capital, Dhaka, where lots of people live in a small area. Bangladesh is also known as "the Land of Rivers", with more than 700 rivers flowing through the lush, green land, helping with travel and farming. But riverbanks can overflow, and even though Bangladesh produces only 0.3% of global greenhouse gas emissions, it is one of the countries most vulnerable to the devastating impacts of climate change, like flooding.

Green, Everywhere!

Bangladesh is carpeted with paddy fields and farms. Rice, vegetables, tea, and fruits like mangoes and coconuts grow here. Jute fibre (used to make twine and rope for weaving), is one of the main exports. Beautiful nature reserves are home to wildlife like the Bengal tiger, fishing cat, and deadly king cobra! Sundarban Reserve Forest is the largest mangrove forest in the world and a UNESCO World Heritage Site.

Sacred Flow

Rivers are not just important for daily life here – they hold deep religious meaning. The Padma (also known as the Ganges) and the Jamuna (also known as the Brahmaputra) are sacred in the Hindu faith, which states that bathing in them can wash away sins. People often hold religious ceremonies by their banks, celebrating both nature and spirituality.

FAST FACTS

Official Name: People's Republic of Bangladesh

Capital: Dhaka

Location: South Asia

Border Countries: India, Myanmar

Official Language: Bengali

Currency: Taka

Population: 173.5 million

Area: 148,460 km^2

MARiNA TABASSUM

Busy City Life

Dhaka is one of the busiest cities in all of South Asia. It's full of energy, with street-food vendors on every corner, malls and a variety of markets for shopping, historic temples and high-rise buildings, and lots of rickshaws weaving through the packed streets. By 2050, Dhaka will be the second-biggest city in the world.

Floating Flower

The beautiful water lily is the national flower of Bangladesh, appearing in local art, literature, and religious imagery. The water lily's bright white or pink petals are often associated with purity and enlightenment in Buddhist and Hindu traditions. The flowers symbolize rebirth because their petals close at night and reopen in the morning.

Did you know?

The jackfruit is the national fruit of Bangladesh.

Spicy Delights

Bangladeshi food is often spicy and full of flavour. It is influenced by Indian cuisine, Bengali culture, and the seasons. Bangladesh recognizes six separate seasons: *grismo* (summer), *barsha* (monsoon), *sharat* (autumn), *hemanto* (late autumn), *sheet* (winter), and *bashonto* (spring), and each comes with its own dishes.

Architecture in Action

Islam is the main religion in Bangladesh, and mosques are an important part of the country's architecture. The modern, light-filled Bait Ur Rouf mosque in Dhaka was designed by Bangladeshi architect Marina Tabassum. Her award-winning work has also addressed the need for safe housing for people affected by flooding. The affordable "Khudi Bari" house is light and high above the ground, and can be quickly dismantled, moved, and rebuilt – without the need for electricity – if a flood hits.

REBEL GIRLS OF BANGLADESH

Bengali feminist thinker, writer, educator, and political activist **Begum Rokeya** (b. 1880) was a pioneer of women's liberation in Bangladesh and India. She fought for fair education for women and girls.

Wasfia Nazreen (b. 1982) is a mountaineer, activist, environmentalist, social worker, and writer. She was the first Bengali and Bangladeshi person to scale K2, the world's second-highest peak.

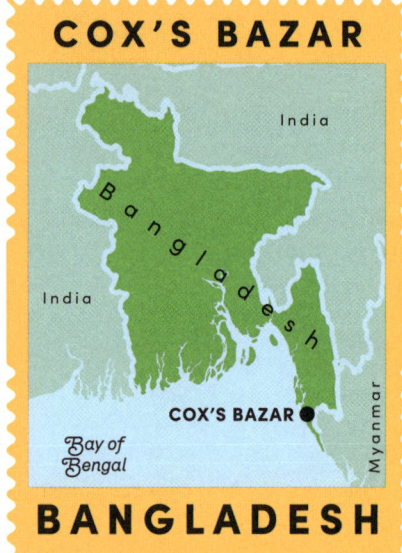

COX'S BAZAR, BANGLADESH

Age: *13*

My home:
I live with my mother, father, and my three sisters, Anamika (25), Maruya (22), and Zamzam (21). We speak Bengali. I share my bedroom with my mum. It has an en suite. I have decorated the walls with paper flowers that I made, and my drawings. We have a wardrobe and a reading table, which I love most of all.

My village:
I live in a rural village in Cox's Bazar district. I love walking here alone in the morning, when it's still quiet. I enjoy the morning sun and the sweet breeze. There are trees on both sides of the road. I love listening to the birds chirping. I can see chickens wandering around and paddy fields spread across the horizon.

Sumaiya

People call me Babu

Every morning I wake to the sound of Azan, the call to prayer for Muslims. I do my morning prayers and read The Holy Quran. Mum makes me an early breakfast because I join coaching support at school from 7am. Classes begin at 10am. I have coaching after school, too. After evening Azan, I return home to freshen up, do my evening prayers, and start my homework. I walk to and from school, but on weekends, when I visit my relatives, we ride in a motorized rickshaw.

My favourite subject is science. I love doing equations, as well as practical experiments. I want to become a doctor when I'm older so I can help the people in my village. We don't have any doctors nearby. We have to travel to the city when we need to see one, and it is a hassle. I want to treat people for free, especially those in need.

My mother cooks *biryani* for special occasions, like when I do well in exams or when we entertain guests. When I feel happy, I ask my mum to cook it. The entire house fills up with the most amazing smell. Every few minutes I go to the kitchen to ask Mum when it will be ready, and I get a little taste from the pot!

We have a cat called Litu. He is a small white kitten who turned up at our house one day. He comes running to me when I come back from school. He waits under the table when I sit down to eat, and I share my food with him. He sometimes climbs onto my lap.

Reading and travelling are my passions. Books can take me to new places without leaving my village! I was a book captain at my primary school. I used to help my friends select and check out books from our class library. Reading became a habit that I still enjoy.

"If you keep calm and explain yourself to others politely, they will usually be supportive."

Mim

My family calls me Akhi

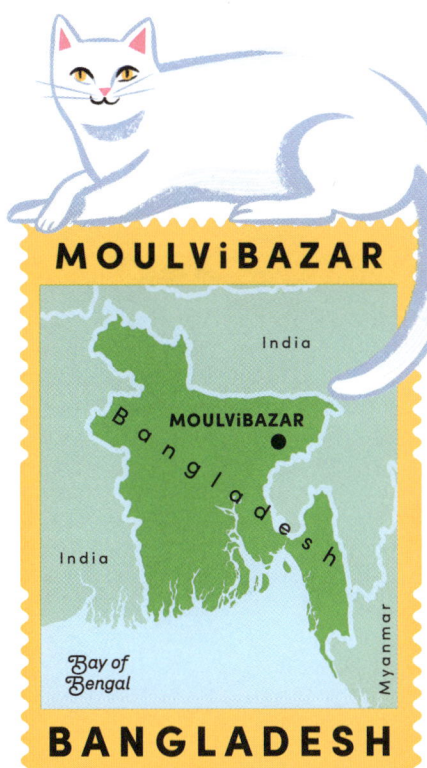

As Muslims we celebrate two Eids every year. We get to wear new dresses and Mum prepares delicious dishes. Relatives and neighbours come to visit, and we all share food, play, and chat. I also enjoy *Waz-Mahfil*, a Bangladeshi preaching event where we gather to hear speeches on Islamic culture and practices. *Alems* (religious scholars) come to my village from different parts of the country. I enjoy listening to them and learning more about my faith.

My friends and I are in a Life Skills club, run by *Room to Read*. Our clubroom has footballs, skipping ropes, and board games for us to enjoy. We chat about movies, what's happening at home, or books we've read. After school, we sometimes go to splash around in the waterfall in the hills near my house. The water is so clean and clear you can even drink from it.

REBEL GIRL SUPERPOWER: SPEAKING UP WHEN I SEE INJUSTICE

I love watching movies and TV shows. My hobby is acting out the characters for my friends; I imagine myself as one of them. I love watching football, too.

For special occasions I wear salwar kameez. If the event has a lot of people, I wear a burqa over it. I have a few to choose from. I like wearing shirts and trousers, too. I have a favourite black T-shirt that has a doll on it that I wear at home.

I have visited our local tea garden a few times. It is very green and beautiful. You can see row upon row of small tea trees planted in a vast area. Workers carry a big bag on their backs, and some of them hang it from their head. For tea, the two top leaves and the leaf buds at the tips of the stems are picked and taken to the factory. It's amazing to see 30 to 50 people picking tea leaves in one place.

Age: 12

My home:
I live with my parents, my younger sister, Laaki (8), and our cute white cat, Rocky. My brother went abroad to work. We speak Bengali, with a Sylheti dialect. I share my room with my mother and my younger sister. It is medium sized with tin walls and a roof. We have a bed, a TV, and a reading table in front of the window where I do my homework. I like to keep it organized!

My village:
I live in a remote, hilly, tree-lined village in the Moulvibazar district, which has some of the highest tea gardens in Bangladesh. I love the cool breeze and the peace and quiet in the hills at dawn.

Cambodia

Cambodia is known for awe-inspiring architecture, glorious national parks, and rare wildlife, like the Sun Bear. Tourism is Cambodia's main industry, and the country is also known for exporting clothes, rubber, rice, and wood. The capital city, Phnom Penh, has a mix of modern and historic buildings, but Cambodia's most famous landmark is Angkor Wat, a huge Hindu–Buddhist temple complex, which is the largest religious site in the world.

Did you know? Long-tailed macaque monkeys are an endangered species, but they live abundantly around Ankor Wat.

FAST FACTS

Official name: Kingdom of Cambodia

Capital: Phnom Penh

Location: Southeast Asia

Official Language: Khmer

Currency: Riel

Border Countries: Laos, Thailand, Vietnam

Population: 17.6 million

Area: 181,035 km²

Ancient Angkor Wat

Angkor Wat was built at the height of the ancient Khmer Empire in the 12th century CE. It started off as a Hindu temple honouring the god Vishnu, before becoming a place of Buddhist worship. The enormous Angkor Wat complex was so carefully designed that twice a year, on the spring and autumn equinox, the sunrise aligns perfectly with the temple's central tower! Angkor Wat is famous for the extraordinary decoration on its outer wall, a masterpiece of intricate stone carvings that stretch for around 700 metres. It took decades for the artists to finish their work, which includes scenes from an epic battle between the Hindu gods and demons.

Local Delicacies

A typical Cambodian dish is *amok*, a creamy fish curry made with coconut milk and served on banana leaves. Noodles, rice, and fresh fruits like mangoes and bananas are also popular, as is street food like grilled skewers of meat, including crickets, tarantulas, and worms.

Floating Villages

The floating village communities on the Tonlé Sap lake have developed a unique way of life. However, most people living in these waterborne homes are vulnerable to environmental issues caused by the climate crisis, like drought or storms. The "She Is The Answer" project, which started in 2021, trains local women to tend floating vegetable gardens, growing crops like cabbages that can be sold as well as eaten.

Celebrations

The people of Cambodia celebrate many festivals,. Pchum Ben is a time for families come together and honour the souls of their ancestors by making offerings at monasteries and pagodas. The water festival Bon Om Touk marks the end of the monsoon season with dragon boat racing and fireworks.

NOU SREY POV

Sporting Success

The national sport of Cambodia is Kun Khmer, a martial art that requires athletes to be tough, flexible, and very nimble. Each fight begins with a sacred dance ritual to show respect to all the people who have supported both fighters, then lasts for either 3 or 5 rounds of 3 minutes. The winner is decided by a knockout, or by winning the most points. Its roots are in an ancient martial art that was immortalized in the stone carvings of Angkor Wat. Now, many centuries later, modern Kun Khmer is streamed on social media and shown on TV! Fans can tune in to admire the talents of fighters like the Cambodian world champion of 2018, Nou Srey Pov, who had her first Kun Khmer fight at just 13 years old.

REBEL GiRLS OF CAMBODiA

Queen Indradevi (b. 1181) of the Khmer Empire influenced important aspects of how the empire was run, and was also active as a poet and a professor of three temple schools.

Entrepreneur **Vannary San** started sustainable fashion company Lotus Silk with one sewing machine. Her company provides employment opportunities for women from disadvantaged communities.

KAMPONG CHHNANG
CAMBODIA

Age: 8

My home:
I live with my father, mother, and grandmother. Our house has two bedrooms: one for my parents and one for my grandmother, so I share with my grandmother. The room is small so we share a bed.

My village:
I live in a rural village in the Kampong Chhnang province of central Cambodia. Although it is a small place, a lot of people live here. There is a market where my grandmother buys food every day. There is a pagoda and a school where I go to study.

"I don't have any pets because my grandmother worries they might bite!"

Linka

Village games are so fun!

We speak Khmer at home and at school. My nickname in Khmer is Sreyneath. It means "prosperity" or "good fortune" in Cambodian culture.

My grandmother takes me to school every day. I wear a uniform. When I arrive, I help to clean the classroom with my friends. We water the flowers before lessons begin. We do exercises in class and read books. At break time, we play hopscotch. When I get home, I do my homework, read more books, and do extra exercises if I have time.

I want to be a teacher when I'm older. I want to be as smart as my grandmother and to teach children about the world. I enjoy reading all sorts of books from my school library, especially ghost stories and funny stories. My mother and grandmother buy me books, too.

I feel proud when my teacher praises me – for being smart, brave, and having good handwriting. My grandmother and my mother have always encouraged me to study hard to get good grades. My favourite subjects are Khmer and maths because I like reading and doing sums.

The whole village plays games at Khmer New Year. Bos Angkunh involves getting into two teams at the pagoda and taking turns to throw the dried brown seeds of the *angkunh* fruit to break the other team's seed formation. To play Chol Chhoung we throw a knotted scarf high up into the air, trying to hit a player from the opposing team. If anyone drops it the whole village breaks into dance and song!

I like to eat *prahok*, which is a salted and fermented fish paste, often made from snakehead fish. I eat it with stir-fried vegetables. I eat a lot of rice, too. I help to cook it at home. I also wash the dishes, help with laundry, and sweep the house.

REBEL GIRL SUPERPOWER

MY NEAT HANDWRITING

Dalin

Everybody calls me Pin!

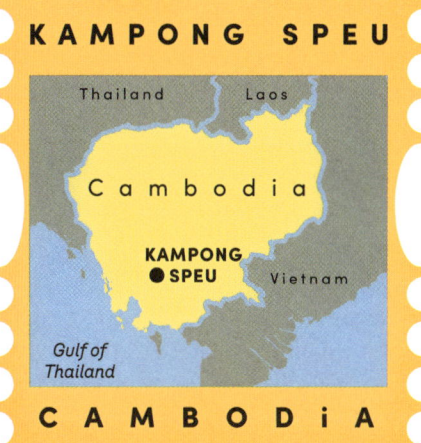

I love school, but I often have to stay at home to help – either with household chores or assisting my father with his bread business. I help by washing the clothes and dishes, cleaning and organizing the house, and preparing dipping sauces and pickles for my father to sell. I prefer to wear short-sleeved shirts and knee-length shorts for ease of doing chores. For special occasions, I wear long dresses or jeans.

Getting good results at school makes me feel proud. Khmer language, history, and science are my favourite subjects. In grade seven, I was a member of the maths club; we solved difficult problems.

Kampong Speu is famous for palm sugar, which is made from palm-tree sap. The palm tree is a very important resource in my province as its trunk can be used to build houses and make utensils, its leaves can be used for roofing, and its sap is used for making sugar and vinegar.

We tend to eat rice with fried meat. Or we'll have soup, bread, or sticky rice cakes. We drink sugar-cane juice or water. I also like Samlor Korko, which is a traditional Cambodian soup made with vegetables. Nom Banh Chok are lightly fermented rice noodles, typically eaten for breakfast here. We also eat a lot of *amok* (steamed fish curry).

Laughing with family and friends makes me happiest. I love chatting to my friends about anything and everything, and I also love exercising. My favourite sports are football and volleyball because they enable Cambodians to compete internationally and make our country known.

Age: 13

My home:
I live with my father, mother, grandmother, and sister, Voleak (18). We all speak Khmer. We have two cats and two dogs. I have my own room. My study desk is my favourite thing in it; I have repurposed bottle caps to make pen holders to keep it tidy. I always like to check my timetable and prepare my books for the next day.

My village:
I live in a busy, rural village in central Cambodia. It comes to life in the morning with people preparing to go to work in factories, and farmers raising their cattle, chickens, and ducks. There are small traders and government officials in the village, too. I ride on the back of a motorcycle to get around.

REBEL GIRL SUPERPOWER: MY PERSEVERANCE. I ALWAYS TRY TO DO MY BEST

"I'd love to be a police officer, to bring justice to the community and eliminate discrimination."

China

The Great Wall
Did you know that some of the mortar used to bind the Great Wall of China's stones was made with sticky rice? A UNESCO World Heritage Site, the Great Wall winds through the north of China like a dragon. It is the longest human-made structure ever built, stretching a distance of more than 20,000 kilometres. It was built over the course of a thousand years, beginning in 220 BCE, to protect ancient China from invaders.

The People's Republic of China is a global superpower and home to a fifth of the world's people, living in cities like Beijing and Shanghai, and in rural communities. It is the world's biggest exporter of goods and its huge factories provide income for the country and jobs for its people. The majority of the population are Han Chinese – descendants of people who settled here more than 5,000 years ago. Sites like the Great Wall and Terracotta Army are reminders of its rich and long-lasting culture.

FAST FACTS

Official Name: People's Republic of China

Capital: Beijing

Location: East Asia

Official Languages: Standard Chinese, Mandarin

Currency: Yuan Renminbi

Border Countries: Afghanistan, Bhutan, India, Kazakhstan, Kyrgyzstan, Laos, Mongolia, Myanmar, Nepal, North Korea, Pakistan, Russia, Tajikistan, Vietnam.

Population: 1.41 billion

Area: 9.6 million km²

Chinese Zodiac
Chinese astrology is popular all around the world. Each year of the Chinese zodiac is represented by one of 12 animals: the rat, ox, tiger, rabbit, dragon, snake, horse, goat, monkey, rooster, dog, and pig. Your sign is the animal that represents the year you were born, and you are said to have personality traits associated with that animal. People born in the year of the horse are said to be free-spirited, energetic, and independent, while those born in the year of the goat are said to be gentle, kind, and creative.

Land of Inventions

Ancient China was much more advanced than many other countries in the world in the areas of science, technology, maths, and astronomy. It is credited with the invention of paper (100 CE), printing (600 CE), and the compass (200 BCE), revolutionizing both communication and navigation. The Chinese also invented kites and fireworks about 3,000 years ago. Today's China remains at the heart of the tech world, leading the way in AI and blockchain technology from super cities like Shanghai, Beijing, and Shenzhen.

Did you know? Ice cream was invented in China in 200 BCE!

Made in China

The world has been consuming products made and exported by China for centuries. First, it was tea, made from leaves mainly planted in the Yangtze River Delta. Porcelain was invented in China long before the rest of the world learned the technique, and was much more advanced than what Europeans in particular were used to, so they imported huge amounts and called it "white gold". China's manufacturing industry continues today in vast factories, making everything from furniture to bags made from recycled plastic bottles.

SHANGHAi

Panda-monium

The Chinese government has been investing resources into the conservation of the country's giant panda population by establishing and extending wildlife reserves. China now has a network of 67 reserves across the country, which protect more than 66 per cent of the giant pandas in the wild.

Confucius

Many values of Chinese society are built on the teachings of a government official called Confucius (*Kongfuzi/Kongzi*), who practised his teachings nearly 3,000 years ago. His philosophy encourages people to treat others with kindness and respect, especially elders; to become a better person through education; to set a good example; and to always do the right thing.

REBEL GiRLS OF CHiNA

Yuan Yuan Tan (b. 1976) is a former principal dancer with the San Francisco Ballet. Her contributions to ballet have been widely recognized and in 2002 she was awarded the prestigious Benois de la Danse award.

Feminist poet and formidable women's activist, **Qiu Jin** (b. 1875), championed the liberation of Chinese women. Through her powerful words, Qiu is remembered for challenging social and gender norms.

Tingxi

Everyone calls me Lulica

Age: 10

My home:
I live with my father, my mother, and our two cats, Pulala and Dafu. Pulala enjoys being treated like a human; she loves to listen in on conversations, so we have to be careful not to speak ill of her. Dafu has a hearty appetite, and he prefers drinking from the tap. My bedroom at home is decorated with handmade crafts, photos, and souvenirs that I've collected from our travels. The walls are covered in my paintings, mostly of my cats!

My city:
I live in Beijing, the capital of China. I walk to school, which is only 10 minutes away. On weekends, we drive to the suburbs or take the tube into the city. We have a lot of stray cats in our neighbourhood. I once worked with my dad to create two cat shelters for them by decorating cardboard boxes, providing them with a cosy haven throughout the winter.

I eat eggs with a steamed stuffed bun for breakfast. Our school lunches are good. We eat rice, vegetables, meat, soup, or fruit. I eat simple dinners with my family in the evening. Sometimes we make Western dishes like pasta or roasted vegetables, and sometimes it's Chinese dishes like dumplings or pancakes. Dumplings are my favourite!

Chinese New Year brings the entire family together. We share a reunion meal, wrap dumplings, watch the Spring Festival Gala, and stay up late. Dressing in traditional Han-style clothing, strolling through temple fairs, and crafting lanterns are also part of the fun. I always wear my traditional *Mamianqun*, also known as a red "horse-face" skirt.

The character "中" (*zhōng*) holds important meaning. In Chinese culture, it can refer to a central position in space, a balanced point in time, or a state of perfect harmony and moderation. Examples include "中正" (fairness), and "中心" (centre). It reflects the ideal of balance in all aspects of life.

Gem hunting is my passion. My parents take me to national parks to admire the wildlife, but what I love most is the rocks! I found several beautiful orange crystals at the Xichou National Stone Desert Park in Yunnan province. I love the nature at Dianchi Lake. It is teeming with red-beaked gulls and is bordered by aquatic fir forests.

I'm on the school cheerleading squad. I attend Latin dance classes every weekend, and during the holidays, I often try escape rooms with friends from my art class. Recently, I have also started learning Baishou gesture dance. Each elegant hand gesture stands for a different part of life. You string the gestures all together to tell a story.

REBEL GIRL SUPERPOWER
BEING UNIQUELY ME

"I'm quite knowledgeable about minerals and gemstones, thanks to a visual handbook my dad bought for me."

Jingyi

My nickname is Hypatia

We study very hard at school, with minimal breaks to play. When I get the chance, I enjoy drawing with my friends at break. I like drawing manga characters because I love reading manga books! I'd love to be a cartoonist when I'm older. I'm passionate about the arts.

I like the Qingming Festival, which is when we visit the graves of our ancestors. We make ritual offerings to them and clean their gravesites. I go with my family to visit my grandpa's grave, then we eat delicious green dumplings and listen to stories about our family. Family is important to me; I take the subway to visit my grandma every weekend.

I enjoy practising Chinese calligraphy. Each character stands for a whole word or concept. There are more than 50,000 of them to learn how to draw. We follow a particular order and the rhythm of the strokes is important. Traditionally, an ink stick, an inkstone (for grinding ink), and a brush are used to prepare ink and paint characters onto paper or silk. The characters are the same in all Chinese dialects.

My nickname is Hypatia, after the ancient Egyptian philosopher and mathematician. She is one of my inspirations, along with my grandma. Hypatia was a persuasive and influential speaker. Students came from all over to learn maths and astronomy from her at a time when women and girls were not well educated.

I'm part of a Twister Stick club at school, and I like to spend time practising gymnastics moves like cartwheels and handstands. I play the guitar, too, and I always wear my blue dress when I'm playing in public.

Age: 11

My home:
I live with my mum and my dad. We speak Mandarin. I have a small room with a bed, a desk, and many books on the shelves. I decorate the walls with the drawings I'm most proud of. We have a cat named Tiger. He is cute, quiet, and fat. He came to be one of our family members when he was just three months old. The markings on his body look just like numbers.

My city:
I live in Shanghai. It is a huge, busy city on China's central coast. People can lead a quiet and easy life in Shanghai. You can find delicious food in small diners on the streets. Even though it's busy, you can drink tea and eat sweet pastries in the gardens hidden in the lanes.

"I try to persuade adults to accept my opinions that differ from theirs."

REBEL GIRL SUPERPOWER: BEING PERSUASIVE

Yihuan Cao

My friends call me CaiCai

Age: 12

My home:
I live with my mother and father. We speak a Shanghai dialect of Chinese at home, and Mandarin at school. I share a room with my parents. Although it's not very big, we make the most of the space and keep it cosy. My favourite thing in it is a lotus lantern that glows at night, creating a warm and peaceful atmosphere.

My city:
I live in Shanghai. It's such a cool city! We also have a home in Nanjing, which is a beautiful old city further up the Yangtze River. I have my own room there, which I find really special. I love my goldfish plant! It's a cute little hanging plant with flowers, and I've been taking care of it for a while now. It makes my room feel so cosy and full of nature!

We live near the biggest skatepark in the world. It's the perfect place for anyone who loves skateboarding, like me. There are so many different ramps and bowls, it never gets boring! I love the challenge and freedom it offers me. When I'm trying difficult tricks, even if I fall or get hurt, I keep pushing myself.

One word in Chinese that I love is "开心" (kāi xīn), which means "fun". But to me, "开心" is more than just simple joy – it's the deep sense of happiness that comes from fully immersing yourself in something, gaining a sense of achievement and fulfillment along the way. It's a joy that stems from focus, dedication, and growth.

We climbed Mount Huangshan recently – a mountain in southern Anhui province, famous for its views. The misty clouds made the landscape look magical, like something out of a fairy tale. There was a rock shaped a bit like a monkey. I even asked it, "Aren't you cold?" It was such a funny and memorable moment.

My school provides a bento box for lunch, and I add some meat soup, eggs, and beef for extra nutrition. If I have skateboard training, I eat something before and after to keep my energy up. Dinner typically includes meat and vegetables, with noodles or rice cakes as the main dish. I like to have a cup of yoghurt before bed.

I like to be creative, whether through drawing, playing the bass, or cooking! I'm part of the creative ensemble club at school. Last summer, we formed a big orchestra of about 70 students and we all rehearsed together for a big performance. Art is my favourite school subject because I love expressing myself.

REBEL GIRL SUPERPOWER: I CAN DRAW WITH BOTH HANDS!

Shi Guiting

Call me Tingting!

We speak Dong ethnic language at home, and learn in Mandarin at school. The character "躲" (*duǒ*) means "to hide" in Standard Chinese but means "beans" in my dialect! I love the traditional clothing of my ethnic group, the Dong. Here, we usually wear it to celebrate people's weddings, as a way to show our support.

The Guzang Festival is important to the Dong and Miao minorities. It is a folk festival that is only held once every seven years for the Dong people, and every thirteen years for the Miao people. On this day, everyone wears traditional clothing and gathers at a public performance space in the village, forming a circle to sing and dance.

I have a long school day. I arrive at 7:20am for morning reading. I have four morning lessons, followed by lunch, which is provided by the school. After lunch, I get to enjoy a nap. In the afternoon, there are four more lessons, and then I have dinner and some relaxation time, followed by evening study until 9:30pm when I head home.

I'm really proud of having a great singing voice. I can remember songs after hearing them once, and I can identify the pitch of instruments without a reference pitch. This might be due to growing up in the homeland of the Kam Grand Choirs – an important part of our Dong heritage. They feature impressive multipart harmonies.

Water buffaloes are special to my region's culture, which is known for its bullfighting tradition. The water buffalo represents the family's honour and prosperity. My village also has a wild passion for football! They have even organized a village football league.

Age: **13**

My home:
I live with my mum and my little sister. My little sister and I share a bedroom. The room has two big shelves for storing clothes, a bed, and a desk for studying. My favourite item is a savings jar that sits by my bed.

My village:
I live in a beautiful village in Guizhou province, which is in a mountainous area of southwest China. It's known for its rural villages, inhabited by minority groups like mine – the Dong. My village is full of warmth and hospitality; the Dong people are friendly and welcoming. My province is also famous for the 74-metre-high Huangguoshu Waterfall, and Dragon Palace Cave, an incredible network of underground waterways.

"I enjoy playing badminton with my friends."

India

Welcome to the most populous country on Earth, the birthplace of some of the world's oldest religions, and the world's fastest growing economy. India has more than 50 cities with populations over a million people. Outside of the cities, the landscape is varied, from the Himalayas in the north to the beautiful beaches in the south, with large rivers such as the Ganges and the Yamuna weaving through the country. Its fertile plains provide abundant crops, like rice and sugarcane.

Did you know? In 2023, India became the first country to land a spacecraft in the Moon's south pole region.

Spiritual Nation

Some of the world's oldest religions started in India, including Hinduism, Buddhism, Jainism, and Sikhism. Today, Hinduism is the main religion, although more than 20 major religious festivals are observed every year by different faith groups. Diwali, the Hindu festival of lights, is celebrated by more than one billion Indians. During Holi, Hindus throw brightly coloured powder at each other to celebrate the beginning of spring. During the Buddhist festival Ullambana, people celebrate family and ancestors by offering food and drink to their ghosts, who visit Earth at this time.

FAST FACTS

Official Name: Republic of India

Capital: New Delhi

Location: South Asia

Official Languages: Hindi, English, Bengali, Tamil, and 18 others

Currency: Rupee

Border Countries: Afghanistan, Bangladesh, Bhutan, China, Myanmar, Nepal, Pakistan

Population: 1.45 billion

Area: 3.3 million km²

Yoga in India

Originating in India more than 5,000 years ago, yoga is still an important part of daily life for many Indians. Yoga breaks are common at school and work; these 10–15 minute sessions focus on breathing techniques and stretches to reduce stress and improve mental clarity.

Bollywood Blockbusters

Based in Mumbai, Bollywood is one of the largest film industries in the world. It produces more than 1,500 films every year – even more than Hollywood. Bollywood films are known for their colourful costumes, catchy music, and elaborate dance scenes. Bollywood films cover all genres, including romance, drama, action, and comedy.

The Taj Mahal

One of the most famous landmarks in the world, the Taj Mahal is located in Agra, India. It was commissioned in 1631 by Emperor Shah Jahan, the 5th Mughal Emperor, in memory of his wife, Mumtaz Mahal. It is made of beautiful white marble and took more than 20 years to complete. The Taj Mahal is a symbol of love and is visited by millions of people every year.

Beautiful Birds

India has over 100 national parks and over 550 wildlife sanctuaries, all teeming with animals, from Indian rhinos to pythons. This is a bird-watchers' paradise, with beautiful, bright birds like the Himalayan monal and Indian pitta soaring the skies. Down on the ground, you might spot the national bird: proud Indian peafowl (peacocks and peahens) strutting their stuff!

Sporting Nation

Cricket is the most popular sport in India. Millions of fans watch it on TV and attend live matches. The Indian Premier League (IPL) is followed by fans around the world. Football is also popular, especially in cities like Kolkata. Other popular sports include badminton, field hockey, wrestling, and kabaddi, a traditional sport that is played across South Asia.

Many Languages

India's 22 official languages include Hindi, Bengali, Marathi, and Tamil, but more than 1,600 languages are spoken across the country. Hindi has the most speakers, while English is widely understood and used in schools and government. Sanskrit – the classical language of Hindu, Buddhist, and Jainist texts – is one of the oldest recorded languages in the world.

REBEL GIRLS OF INDIA

Growing up surrounded by boys in the peshwa's court, **Lakshmi Bai** (b. 1835) was trained in martial arts. A fierce fighter, at just 22 years of age, she refused to cede the city of Jhansi to the British.

Ishita Malaviya (b. 1990) is India's first professional female surfer. She uses her profile to showcase India's beautiful coast as a surfing destination, breaking social stigmas by inviting girls and young women into the water.

Age: 10

My home:
I live with my mum, my dad, and my sister. We speak Hindi and English at home, and English at school. I share a room with my sister. It's decorated really well. My favourite things in our room are the noticeboard and my bed.

My city:
Mumbai is India's largest city, on the west coast. The Gateway of India stone arch stands on our harbour. Elephanta Island is nearby, where there are ancient cave temples dedicated to the Hindu god, Shiva. Our city is famous for being the heart of the Bollywood film industry.

Siya

Music melts away my stress

"'Holi Mubarak' means 'Happy Holi' in Hindi."

I like my school teachers a lot, and I have a tutor outside of school, too. Private tutoring is very common here. Some kids have one-on-one sessions, and some attend tutoring centres. My tutor is one of the women I am most inspired by. And my mum too, of course!

I love the Hindu festival of Holi, when we celebrate the start of spring. We light a bonfire the night before, and throw shredded coconut and rice onto it as gifts to Brahman (god). When we wake up, the real fun starts! We cover our friends and family in brightly coloured powder and water. Holi is a time of fun. People play pranks to celebrate the playful god, Krishna. Legend has it that he played a trick on a group of milkmaids by covering them in coloured water.

I want to be a vet when I'm older. I love animals and want to take care of them all. I used to have a pet fish called Chom, who died recently. Chom was energetic and playful and just a little bit greedy! Whenever I came home from school he would swim around excitedly, looking for me to sprinkle his feed into the tank.

I am interested in how other people think. That's why I love reading. I especially enjoy fantasy fiction and graphic novels. I found the *Cat Kid Comic Club* series by Dav Pilkey so funny. I also read Hindu mantra books like *The Hanuman Chalisa* to keep my mind calm. It is a hymn in praise of the god Hanuman, which you recite aloud. Hanuman's shape is half-monkey half-human. He uses his powers to help others.

I love listening to music, especially hip-hop, K-pop, and pop music. It always puts me in a good mood – it melts away any stress and leaves me ready to dance! I also enjoy playing football and basketball, or just chatting and playing with my friends. When I'm not feeling as energetic I love to draw.

Aadya

My nickname is Aadu

"I love walking and chatting with my best friend. We talk about everything under the sun."

My daily meals usually consist of typical Indian food, like pulses, chapati, pickle, rice, and salad. My favourite Indian food is *rajma chawal*, a type of North Indian curry made with red kidney beans, served with chutney. I love the blend of spices with the zesty flavour of the chutney.

I enjoy the festival of Lohri. It is celebrated in January to mark the harvest of Rabi crops like wheat and mustard, which grow through the winter. To celebrate Lohri we light a bonfire to warm the winter day, and we eat sweet treats made with sesame seeds, like *gajjak* (sesame brittle) and *revadi* (sweets made with jaggery, a sweetener made from palm sap).

I'm happiest when reading and writing. I write poetry and short stories in my diary. I'm in a writing club at school where most of us have become authors using a creative writing platform that allows us to publish books online and sell printed-on-demand books. My book, *Weathered Tales*, is about a young orphan boy who has the power of controlling the weather. I would love to be a professional author one day.

The beauty of our generation is that we question things. I am adamant to find answers any way I can. I love to know about the roots of people. That's why social studies is one of my favourite subjects. Everybody has their own way of seeing the world. I'm always interested to learn more about other people's life philosophies.

I love to play and watch cricket, one of the most famous sports in our country. And I go and exercise in a nearby fitness club every other day. I like to be comfy and my favourite outfits are a loose pair of shorts with a T-shirt in the summer, or cosy pyjamas in the winter. I wear fancy clothes for special occasions, be it Indian or Western dress.

Age: 13

My home:
I live with my mum, my dad, and my brother, Aarav (7). I share a room with Aarav. It is nice and simple, with peach-coloured walls, a photo of us in the centre of the back wall, a study table, and our cupboards. We speak Hindi at home and Hindi and English at school.

My city:
I live in the huge city of Delhi. It is famous for its scrumptious food, like *chole-bhature* (a spicy chickpea curry that is served with leavened fried bread), and its architectural marvels, like Qutub Minar and Lal Qila (the Red Fort). We have lots of street dogs roaming around our area. We feed one of them, who has become a part of our daily lives, always waiting for us with a wagging tail and bright eyes.

Japan

Welcome to Japan: the string of more than 14,000 islands on the eastern edge of Asia. Four main islands make up most of the country, connected by a series of bridges and undersea tunnels. Its mountainous land sits on the Pacific Ring of Fire, where many tectonic plates meet, making Japan incredibly prone to earthquakes. Its highest peak, Mount Fuji, is an active volcano. Most people live in busy cities, where ancient traditions exist side by side with exciting technology.

Respect for Nature

According to Japan's native religion – Shinto – mountains, volcanoes, forests, and waterfalls have their own souls and are considered sacred. Nature's beauty is deeply respected. Every spring, when the *sakura* (cherry blossom) blooms, people enjoy the *hanami* custom of admiring the magical pink wonderlands until the petals drop. Japan's *onsen* (hot springs) are places where bathers can relax in warm, mineral-rich water.

Traditional Hobbies

In Japanese culture, there are some strong connections to the customs of the past. Origami, the Japanese art of paper folding, continues to be a cherished craft, passed down through families. The traditional hours-long tea ceremony is practised as a hobby. If a tea pillar stands up in the cup, it is a lucky omen for the drinker!

FAST FACTS

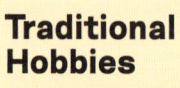

Capital: Tokyo

Location: East Asia

Main islands: Hokkaido, Honshu, Kyushu, Okinawa, Shikoku

Official Language: Japanese

Currency: Japanese Yen

Population: 124 million

Area: 377,915 km²

TOKYO

Tokyo Tech

Japan's neon-lit capital, Tokyo, lies on its biggest island, Honshu. The city is densely populated and people tend to live in small spaces. Tech is a way of life for many of Tokyo's residents, who might enjoy a lunch served to them by robots, or take the famously rapid bullet train to visit a 24-hour unstaffed sweet shop. AI systems, 3D cameras, and weight sensors track customers and the items they select in the shop, without the need for humans.

Healthy Diet

A diet high in fish and rice may be one of the reasons why the Japanese have among the longest life expectancies in the world. Did you know slurping your noodles is considered a sign of appreciation for the chef in Japan? It is said to help you to enjoy the flavours fully. Sweet Japanese treats like *mochi* (brightly coloured steamed rice cakes) are traditionally eaten around New Year.

Sports: Old and New

Sports have long played a significant role in Japanese culture, with martial arts such as judo, karate, and sumo being deeply rooted in tradition. Their practice emphasizes discipline and personal growth. *Yakyū* (baseball), introduced in the 19th century, is also incredibly popular. As well as two professional leagues, the game is played at universities and schools, with high school tournaments attracting massive attention.

Did you know? In the Harajuku area of Tokyo people dress in a distinctive bright style.

Epic Animation

Otaku is the name for Japanese pop culture, like anime, manga, and video games. It has passionate followers around the world. Fans flock to its hub, the Akihabara district of Tokyo, or take a trip to visit the reconstruction of Tokiwa-sō, the apartment building where many manga artists lived and worked together, honing their craft. "*Kawaii*" translates as "adorable" in Japanese and is associated with all things cute, especially cuddly animals with big eyes.

REBEL GiRLS OF JAPAN

Committed to gender equality and the political participation of young people, **Momoko Nojo** (b. 1998) is the founder and director of the NGO NO YOUTH NO JAPAN, which encourages young people to have a political voice.

Keiko Fukuda (b. 1913) was a Japanese-American martial artist, who was the highest-ranked female judoka in history. She is the only woman to have been awarded a 10th-degree black belt in judo.

Meisa

I love manga and anime

Age: 10

My home:
I live with my mum, my dad, my sister, Michiru (8), and my brother, Tokio (4), in a yellow house on a quiet street. We have a beautiful garden and kind neighbours. I share my room with my sister. It is full of teddies!

My city:
We live in Yokohama, Japan's second-largest city. We are just south of Tokyo, on the island of Honshu. We have a zoo, a waterfront park, and Sankeien Garden, which has traditional Japanese landscaping, teahouses, and a three-tiered pagoda.

¶Moving my body and making things make me happy, so PE lessons and arts and crafts are always the highlights of my week. I do horizontal bar and enjoy playing tag rugby after school. I just recently tried badminton and loved it! I like to be creative with cardboard and pens. I am happiest when I can get into the zone, concentrating on my art projects.

"なかよし" (nakayoshi) means friendship in Japanese. My friends and I play a lot of tag and skipping games at school. At the weekend, we go to shops and parks together. I'm lucky to have kind people in my life.

¶I wear my kimono for Children's Day. It's a public holiday dedicated to celebrating the joy of kids and their unique personalities. Families make and decorate *koinobori* (carp-shaped windsocks) and raise them outside so that it looks like the fish are swimming through the air. Each family member has their own fish in a different colour.

We have many autumn festivals in Japan. They celebrate harvests across the country. The Katsuura Festival has such a lively atmosphere! The fishing town hosts four days of events. Colourful *mikoshi* (floats) are carried or drawn by carriages in parades. The smell of local food stalls and the sound of drums, flutes, and energetic shouts from the crowd fill the air. Eventually, the floats are carried into the sea!

¶I want to be a voice actor when I'm older. I love manga and I'm a big fan of Japanese animation, especially *Doraemon* and *Crayon Shin-Chan*. I watched a show about a voice actor on YouTube. He said he loved *Doraemon* and realized that voice acting would allow him to be a part of the story. When I heard that I started to dream of being a part of the story, too.

"Japanese children's author Rieko Nakagawa is one of my heroes."

Kazakhstan

The world's largest landlocked country is also the fourth largest in Asia, with only Russia, China, and India ahead of it in size! Kazakhstan was part of the Soviet Union until the Union collapsed in 1991, and since then, plentiful natural resources have helped its economy to grow. Its landscape ranges from flat, dry *steppe* (grassland) to the peaks of the Tian Shan mountain range. Kazakhstan's deserts include the Aral Sea, which was once one of the largest lakes in the world before it mostly dried up.

Futuristic Capital

Kazakhstan is sparsely populated, which means its people are spread out across a wide area. Most people live in cities, like the super-modern capital, Astana, which is known for its futuristic-looking and tall buildings, including the Bayterek Tower and Khan Shatyr Entertainment Center. Almaty, the biggest city, is famous for its beautiful parks, the nearby Zailiyskiy Alatau mountains, and for being a cultural centre.

Did you know?
The name "Kazakhstan" translates to "Land of the Wanderers", reflecting the nomadic past of its people.

ALMATY

What to spot?
Many national parks and nature reserves protect Kazakhstan's wildlife. In the mountains, you might spot a snow leopard or a wild goat, whereas the deserts are home to Bactrian (two-humped) camels. One of the most famous animals here is the saiga antelope, which is unique to Central Asia, and is known for its funny-looking nose.

FAST FACTS

Official Name: Republic of Kazakhstan

Capital: Astana

Location: Europe, Asia

Official Languages: Kazakh, Russian

Currency: Tenge

Border Countries: China, Kyrgyzstan, Russia, Turkmenistan, Uzbekistan

Population: 20.6 million

Area: 2.725 million km^2

Eating and Drinking

Kazakh food is hearty and often includes meat, especially beef, lamb, and horsemeat. One of the most famous dishes is *beshbarmak*, made of boiled meat, noodles, and onions. Kazakh people also drink a lot of tea, especially green tea, and enjoy a drink called *kumis*, made from fermented mare's milk. A type of bread called *nan* is served with most meals.

Language and Culture

Kazakhstan has two official languages: Kazakh, which is the native language, and Russian, which is also widely spoken. Islam is the largest religion, followed by Eastern Orthodox Christianity. Kazakh people celebrate holidays such as Nauryz, a spring festival that marks the New Year. People play instruments like the *dombra* (a two-stringed guitar-like instrument) and the *kobyz* (a bowed string instrument), and perform Kazakh dances, which are fast-paced and energetic!

Crunch!

The first ever wild apple trees are believed to have grown in the forests of the Tian Shan mountains near Almaty in Kazakhstan. All of the apples that we eat today are ancestors of that first fruit. Scientists believe that Tian Shan apple seeds were first transported out of Kazakhstan by birds and bears, and later by humans through trade. The city of Almaty is often referred to as the "father of apples". It even has an apple-shaped fountain at its centre.

World Nomad Games

Many Kazakh people have ancestors who lived by nomadic customs, moving around the steppe on horseback and herding livestock. In 2024, Astana hosted the 5th World Nomad Games. The city welcomed 3,000 athletes from 89 countries to compete in 21 nomadic activities, many of which are inspired by the survival skills needed for life on the steppe, like horseback archery and hunting with eagles. Kazakhstan won the most medals, and its people were able to connect with their roots through showcases of food, dress, crafts, and music.

REBEL GIRLS OF KAZAKHSTAN

Painter and educator **Aisha Galimbaeva** (b. 1917) used her gift for artistic expression to highlight the position of women in the Soviet Union during the mid-20th century.

Ulzhan Baibussynova (b. 1973) is a *zhyrau*, performing oral poetry while playing the *dombra*. She has inspired a generation of women who are challenging gender boundaries in Kazakh music.

Leisan

Dancing frees my mind

My favourite traditional Kazakh food is *baursak*. It's a type of dough fried in oil, a bit like a doughnut, but not as sweet. I like to eat it with tea and chocolate cream.

I like to celebrate Nauryz, the Kazakh festival marking the beginning of a new year. Celebrations begin on 21 March and last a few days. We play traditional games, wear traditional clothing (brightly coloured dresses, waistcoats, robes, and hats, all with detailed embroidery), and prepare a special broth called Nauryz *kozhe*. It's meant to bring good luck.

Dancing feels like freedom to me. You don't think about anything else when you're dancing except the next step. I'd love to be a pop artist when I grow up, like the members of my favourite K-pop group, BLACKPINK.

We speak Russian at home and at school, but a lot of people in Kazakhstan speak Kazakh, too. There is always an opportunity to learn something new at school, and to achieve new goals. My favourite subject is maths. I'm not in any school clubs, but I keep very busy with my hobbies outside of it!

My favourite sport is swimming. I'm on a swim team and we train three times a week at the local pool before school. When we're together my friends and I like to play games, and we chat about our common interests.

Our family trip to Disneyland is my happiest memory. We went to the one in Hong Kong. It was just amazing! I grew up watching Disney cartoons with my family, so when I saw the characters come to life I felt like I was on cloud nine. At the end of the last day there was an incredible firework show over the Disney castle that lit up the night sky.

Age: **10**

My home:
I live with my mum, my dad, and my brother, Taip (18). I have two brothers who have left home. I share a bedroom with Taip. It has a simple layout with two beds and a table. My favourite thing in it is my night light, which helps me not to be afraid of the dark!

My city:
Almaty is Kazakhstan's largest city, set in the foothills of the Trans-Ili Alatau mountains. It is a wonderful city to live in, with lots of parks and amenities, as well as historic buildings such as Zenkov Cathedral, which has bright blue and yellow spires.

REBEL GIRL SUPERPOWER: TRYING MY BEST

Laos

Welcome to Laos! Officially named Lao People's Democratic Republic (LPDR), it is known for its rugged mountainous landscape, with three-quarters of the land covered by lofty hills and mountains. Laos is the only completely landlocked country in Southeast Asia. Many Laotians are farmers living in rural communities. The golden temples and wide boulevards of the capital, Vientiane, reflect both the country's Buddhist faith and its past under French colonialist rule, which ended in 1953.

Local Produce

Laos has a tropical monsoon climate with a wet season from June to October, creating the perfect environment to grow crops. Bananas, cassava, and coffee are the biggest crop exports, but rice, tea, strawberries, and pineapples are grown here, too. Each community has a lively local market where fresh produce is bought and sold.

FAST FACTS

Official name: Lao People's Democratic Republic (LPDR)

Capital: Vientiane

Location: Southeast Asia

Official Language: Lao

Currency: Lao Kip

Border Countries: Cambodia, China, Myanmar, Thailand, Vietnam

Population: 7.77 million

Area: 236,800 km²

Where in the World?

Laos is sandwiched between Thailand and Vietnam, and bordered by Myanmar, China, and Cambodia. With so many neighbours crossing its borders, it is considered one of the most ethnically diverse countries in mainland Southeast Asia. It has been a communist state since 1975. The main religion is Buddhism.

Celebrating New Year

Lao New Year, also known as Boun Pi Mai, is the most important holiday in the Lao calendar. This three-day festival marks the start of the lunar calendar year. It is a government holiday, and celebrations can last more than a week in some towns!

Places to Visit

Entering the town of Luang Prabang feels like stepping back in time. Once the royal capital of Laos, it is now a UNESCO World Heritage Site, famous for its temples, architecture, and stunning views. The mysterious Plain of Jars is another ancient site, known for its thousands of large stone jars scattered across the landscape. No one knows how or why they were placed there, but they are believed to be more than 2,000 years old.

THE PLAIN OF JARS

Did you know? Laos rhymes with "cow" not "house"!

Land of a Million Elephants

Laos was once known by the name Lan Xang, meaning the "Land of a Million Elephants". It once had a huge population of wild elephants that roamed freely. Now, you are much more likely to come across a water buffalo. In fact, Lao people mostly rear buffalo instead of cows, meaning beef is not common in the local diet.

Life on the River

The Mekong River runs the length of Laos. It is vital for transportation, since the mountains and dense jungle can make travel tricky. The river waters crops and is full of fish, and hydroelectric dams create energy for Laos to use and sell. These dams are controversial though, as they may harm wildlife like the rare Irrawaddy dolphin.

REBEL GIRLS OF LAOS

Writer **Dara Viravong Kanlagna** (b. 1940) explores themes such as the role of women in society and education, and the struggles that some Lao women face as a result of poverty and traditions.

Silina Pha Aphay (b. 1996) is a sprinter from Laos. She was a flag bearer in the Tokyo 2020 Summer Olympic Games Parade of Nations, and holds the national record for Laos in the 100 metres event.

Chitsavanh

Everyone calls me Som

Age: 10

My home:
I live with my father, my grandmother, and one of my aunts. My parents are divorced. I share my bedroom with my grandmother. It is nice and simple; there is a bed, a mosquito net, a picture of my grandfather, and a sacred Buddhist altar, where we can pay our respects to Buddha and to deceased family members.

My village:
I live in a small village in the Luang Prabang province in northern Laos. Our village is near Mount Phousi. Ancient legend tells of a powerful naga (a part-human part-serpent deity in Buddhist tradition), who used to call the mountain home, and there are beautiful little temples and shrines dotted up the hill, with golden rooftops visible through the trees.

"I am determined and I do not give up easily on things."

Our family raises ducks and chickens, and we grow vegetables. Chickens are much harder to catch than dogs! My chores at home include washing dishes, sweeping floors, washing clothes for my grandmother and my father, and feeding our animals.

Pork laab is our national dish. To make it, you fry pork mince with fresh herbs like mint, coriander, and kaffir lime leaves, as well as *galangal* (a root a bit like ginger), spring onions, and fresh lime juice. Some people add toasted ground rice and serve it with crunchy lettuce; other people eat it with sticky rice or on its own. I often eat pork jerky at home, too.

I'm a member of the Children's Cultural Centre in Luang Prabang. I go there to learn traditional Lao and modern dance. The centre provides after-school and weekend activities for Lao children to learn about our culture and traditions through music, drama, storytelling, and a variety of arts and crafts activities.

My friends and I love running races, and playing hopscotch. I enjoy spending time with them at school, sharing meals, and studying together.

I normally wear casual clothes, but I wear a uniform to school and I put on my *sinh* (traditional skirt worn in Laos) when going to temples or festivals like Boun Pi Mai, the Lao New Year festival. We celebrate it in April, which is the fifth lunar month of the Buddhist calendar. It's a fun time of year when we have water fights and attend parades.

I take my education seriously. I love learning languages and I would love to be a doctor when I grow up, like my Aunt Phueng. She inspires me. My Aunt Mou is an inspiration to me too, because she is very entrepreneurial.

REBEL GIRL SUPERPOWER: MY DEDICATION TO LEARNING

Malaysia

Malaysia is separated into two distinct landmasses, divided by the South China Sea. To the west, there's Peninsular Malaysia, which shares land borders with Thailand and Singapore. To the east, there's East Malaysia, which has Brunei to the north and Indonesia to the south. Along its waters, there are just under 900 islands that make up the rest of Malaysia. With thick rainforests, beachy coasts, rolling hills, and steep mountains, the landscape is as varied as the people who live here.

Fantastic Festivals

Because of all the different cultures here, there is a fantastic array of festivals to celebrate, including the Hindu festival of Thaipusam, and the Islamic festival of Eid al-Fitr (or Hari Raya Puasa in the Malay language). On 31 August, there's Hari Merdeka, Malaysia's Independence Day. And in May or June, there's the Dragon Boat Festival, a fun day on which people race boats that are decorated to look like dragons.

Did you know?
Taman Negara National Park is so old that there is evidence to show that dinosaurs once roamed here!

A Wealth of Wildlife

Malaysia is one of the world's mega-diverse countries. That means it has many species that live only here. One animal native to these shores is the orangutan. It's a magnificent, intelligent creature, but due to poaching and destruction of its habitat, it's critically endangered, and conservationists in the country are working hard to protect it. In the seas, there are many turtle species, including hawksbill, green, and leatherback sea turtles.

FAST FACTS

Capital: Kuala Lumpur

Location: Southeast Asia

Official Language: Malay

Currency: Malaysian Ringgit

Border Countries: Brunei, Indonesia, Singapore, Thailand, Vietnam

Population: 35.6 million

Area: 330,803 km²

Malaysian Craft

The Mah Meri people of Malaysia are skilled at carving intricate wooden masks. These masks are used in special ceremonies, such as weddings, and represent the good spirits that the people believe in. They can be sculpted to look like humans or like animals. Another important display of Malaysian craft and ingenuity is the batik textile. Plain cloth is covered in patterns drawn in wax, then dyed. When the wax is removed, it reveals the undyed patterned areas. Malaysian batik often features bright colours and big patterns.

Lush Trees and Pungent Flowers

One of the world's oldest rainforests, dated at more than 130 million years old, can be found in the Taman Negara National Park. There are some fascinating and rare animals here, including the Malayan tiger, the Asian elephant, and the clouded leopard. It's also home to a very stinky inhabitant: *Rafflesia*, the world's largest flower. It has huge red petals spotted with white, and it reeks of rotting meat.

Kuala Lumpur

The largest city in Malaysia, Kuala Lumpur, is also its capital. It is a place of true diversity and there is a huge variety of different cuisines, buildings, and cultures all residing together. Some of the world's tallest buildings are here, including Merdeka 118, which was completed in 2023 and opened in 2024, and is currently the second-tallest building in the world.

Meals of Malaysia

The country's position on the Spice Route – a voyage merchants took to trade goods around the world – provided a wealth of fragrant spices. Today's cuisine also includes influences from the Chinese, Indian, and Indonesian cultures that passed through.

REBEL GiRLS OF MALAYSiA

Adventurer **Anita Yusof** (b. 1968) has crisscrossed the globe on two epic motorcycle journeys, making her the first Muslim woman to ride solo around the world.

Adele Lim (b. 1975) is a screenwriter, producer, and director, known for *Crazy Rich Asians*, *Raya and the Last Dragon*, and *Joy Ride*. She is passionate about supporting a new and increasingly diverse generation of storytellers.

Zi Zhi

I love all things K-pop!

Age: 9

My home:
I live in a big, lively bungalow with my whole extended family! There are eight adults including my parents, grandparents, aunts, and uncles, plus seven kids, including me, my little brother, Aston Lim (7), and our new tiny baby sister, Arynna Lim. We also have a French bulldog, Omnia! I share a bunk bed with my brother (I get the top), and I have my own cosy little corner where I keep my toy collection and my favourite books.

My city:
Kuala Lumpur is Malaysia's capital. It's a fun city with shiny modern buildings, like the iconic Petronas Twin Towers, and ancient temples, like the Sri Mahamariamman. We have huge shopping malls, colourful street markets, yummy food stalls, and parks to play in.

We speak English, Mandarin, and Hokkien dialects at home, and English and Mandarin at school. I travel to school by car with my brother and cousins, who I live with. It's fun talking to them about school and friends we meet. On weekends, we sometimes fly if we're going somewhere special, like Singapore, where my other cousins live. Weekends are my favourite time to explore and have fun!

Nasi lemak is a super tasty Malaysian dish, with coconut rice, spicy sambal, crunchy peanuts, little anchovies (my favourite!), and an egg. I love that it has so many different flavours all on one plate. I also enjoy Korean and Japanese food.

Celebrating Chinese New Year is always fun. We have a big family gathering. We enjoy yummy food, and watch the lion dance. I get red packets filled with money for good luck, which makes it even more special!

I'm in a K-pop group called Pink Queen with my friends. We love performing in competitions together. Singing and dancing makes me feel accomplished and happy, especially when we've worked hard to put on a great show.

My favourite outfits have a K-pop style. I love wearing trendy oversized jackets, graphic tees, and high-waisted trousers with cool accessories. For special occasions, I like to add a bit of sparkle or something unique, like bold colours or fun layers, to really stand out like a K-pop star!

I want to be an Olympic gymnast.
I'm on the school team. It's my dream to perform on the world stage.

"I really love exploring different places and cultures."

Nepal

Nestled high in the Himalayas, Nepal has eight of the world's tallest mountains, including the world's highest: Mount Everest. Its scenery is breathtaking – soaring peaks, crashing waterfalls, and deep valleys shape the landscape. There are around 101 different ethnic groups in Nepal, including the Sherpa people, and the Magar people. Three-quarters of the population are farmers living in the river valleys, growing crops like rice and wheat.

Birthplace of Buddha

Lumbini province is known as the birthplace of Siddhartha Gautama, who later became the Buddha. A beautiful garden, a peaceful pond, and the Maya Devi Temple mark the place where Buddha was born more than 2,500 years ago. People visit to reflect, meditate, and learn about Buddha's teachings of kindness, peace, and enlightenment.

Did you know? The Himalayas are still rising. Mount Everest "grows" five centimetres each year!

The mythical Yeti – also known as the Abominable Snowman – is said to live in the mountains of Nepal!

Highest Place on Earth

Mount Everest (known locally as Sagarmāthā), stands proudly at almost 8,849 metres! Many adventurers, climbers, and trekkers travel to Nepal hoping to reach the world's highest summit. Most of them wouldn't be able to attempt the climb without help from expert Sherpa mountain guides. The Sherpa people are well adapted to life at high altitude and are among the greatest mountaineers in the world.

FAST FACTS

Official Name: Federal Democratic Republic of Nepal

Capital: Kathmandu

Location: South Asia

Official Language: Nepali

Currency: Nepalese Rupee

Border Countries: China, India

Population: 29.6 million

Area: 147,181 km²

Let's Celebrate

Most people practise Hinduism in Nepal, but Buddhism is also practised. Some people observe both religions. Many people visit temples and *stupas* (dome-shaped Buddhist shrines), and there are festivals throughout the year. During Tihar, the fesitval of lights, Hindus in Nepal decorate their homes with bright lights, sing songs and play games. Over the five-day festival, different animals who live alongside humans, like crows, cows, and dogs, are celebrated.

Kathmandu: Heart of Nepal

The capital of Nepal is a busy, thriving city. One of the most famous places to visit is Swayambhunath, known as "the Monkey Temple", where you can see monkeys and a golden stupa. Kathmandu has been called the "living cultural museum of the world" because it has so many ancient places of worship from different faiths.

The Karnali Bridge

This famous bridge is located over the Karnali River. It helps people to travel between remote areas and larger cities, making it easier to trade goods and access services. The views from the bridge are incredible, with the rushing river below and the surrounding mountains. It's a vital piece of infrastructure for the people of Nepal.

Not all Mountains!

Khaptad National Park is known for its greenery and rich biodiversity, with rolling meadows and forests of oak and rhododendron trees. It is home to a variety of animals, from leopards to wild boars. Khaptad is also a spiritual site, with temples and shrines that attract pilgrims.

REBEL GiRLS OF NEPAL

Sujana Rana and **Roja Maya Limbu** faced discrimination as migrant workers in Lebanon in the early 2010s, so they became two of the first worker unionists in the Middle East, fighting for their rights.

Purnima Shrestha (b. 1991) has climbed seven of Nepal's 8,000-metre-plus peaks. She completed them all in four years and eight months, becoming the fastest Nepali woman to do so.

Gurans

I'm proud to work hard!

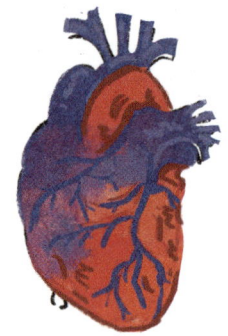

Age: 13

My home:
I live with my dad, my sister, Kusum, and my brother, Prince. My mum lives abroad, in Kuwait. We speak Nepali at home. I share a room with my siblings. The walls are painted sky-blue, and I have hung my certificates and my timetable on them. I love how neat and clean it always is.

My town:
I live in a bustling town in the Banke District of Lumbini province in western Nepal, near the Indian border. We have busy streets, a lot of schools, and a medical college. I usually travel to school in an electric three-wheeled autorickshaw, but sometimes I walk.

¶I want to do something in a health-related field. My dream job is to become a cardiovascular surgeon. I am passionate about science; it helps us to understand the world around us. I would also be interested in social work.

¶I love being a part of group activities. I'm a member of the Scouts and Red Cross clubs, my local Adolescent Girls Club, and my school's Climate Justice Club. I have learned a lot and I try to teach my family, friends, and neighbours that we should keep our environment clean and plant more trees whenever possible. Shreya KC is an inspiring young leader involved in climate change activism in Nepal. She is a role model for young women, raising awareness about climate change.

¶Dashain is one of the biggest festivals in Nepal. It happens around September and falls during the long school holidays. I love how families come together to play cards, fly kites, and eat delicious food. I also visit my relatives to get blessings from them.

¶I mostly eat *dal bhat* (lentils and rice), with mixed vegetable curry. I also drink milk every day. My favourite traditional food is *sel roti*. It is made from rice flour, looks like a donut, and is fried. It is usually made on special occasions.

¶Playing with my siblings makes me happy. Spending time with them, reading books, and watching movies is what makes me smile. I like to play badminton, too. When I'm at home I help with the cooking, and I also help my brother and sister to complete their homework.

Reading inspiring books helps me to learn and grow. They help me to stay focused on my goals, maintain a positive mindset, and always remember my inner potential.

REBEL GIRL SUPERPOWER: MY CURIOSITY ABOUT THE WORLD

"I always want to be the best version of myself."

Subina

I like to make a positive impact

"I love to perform stand-up comedy routines for my friends."

GORKHA MUNICIPALITY
NEPAL

Age: 13

School is a five-minute walk away from home. I enjoy exchanging morning greetings and saying *namaste* ("hello") to my neighbours on the way. At the weekend, I usually stay at home and watch TV, or sometimes I go to the cinema.

I typically eat egg curry with rice and some *achaar*, (a spicy homemade relish), but my all-time favourite dish is *choila*, especially my dad's. It's a smoky, grilled-meat dish: a beloved Newari delicacy that embodies the vibrant flavours of my culture. I also love *Samay Baji*, which is a whole platter of different side dishes for special occasions.

I have tutoring for three hours before school. Our school day starts at 9am and is broken into seven periods of different subjects, each lasting 45 minutes. My favourite subject is Nepali language class. I love literature, especially poetry. I'm allowed to use the library, computer room, or science lab during breaks. My favourite has to be the library, since I get lost inside the worlds of stories.

Scouts is always fun. I am a troupe leader and I love getting to be a part of different community activities and spending time outdoors with my friends. Doing things that make a positive impact in my community makes me happy.

I often help in the kitchen at home. I also fetch the family's drinking water from the stone tap, which I don't enjoy. It takes over an hour to go to the spring and come back again. Sometimes there is a huge queue and I have to wait a long time for my turn to fill the pot.

I want to become a civil engineer. I've seen how new roads and bridges help my community to travel a little more easily than they did before.

My home:
I have a big family, and I love it. I live with my parents, my grandmother, my aunts and uncles, and my brother. We speak Nepali at home. I share a bedroom with my brother and grandmother. There are three beds and two cupboards in it. Mum stores cooking utensils under my bed. The walls are decorated with certificates, my brother's drawings, and a family photo.

My village:
I live in a tiny village, high in the hills. The area is peaceful in the mornings, filled with the soothing sounds of birdsong.

Singapore

Many Cultures
Home to many ethnic and religious groups, Singapore is dotted with temples, mosques, and churches. Buddhism, Hinduism, Christianity, Islam, and Taoism are the main religions. With so many different traditions and festivals, there is always someone celebrating in this happening city!

Singapore is a city, an island, and a country all at once! Starting out as a tiny fishing village, today the city-state of Singapore is a major financial power in Southeast Asia. Officially, the Republic of Singapore is made up of the main island and more than 60 smaller islands, many of which are nature havens, though it is better known for city living and stunning modern architecture. Singapore is a culturally diverse and wealthy country, with one of the highest life expectancies in the world.

Tropical Rain
It rains somewhere in Singapore's islands almost every day of the year. Locals describe its four seasons as: hot, hotter, wet, and wetter! This makes for a lush, rich habitat for water-loving plants such as mangroves, and animals such as monitor lizards, otters, and crocodiles. You can spot them at the Sungei Buloh Wetland Reserve.

Do You Speak Singlish?
Singapore has four official languages: Malay, English, Mandarin Chinese, and Tamil. English is the main language used in schools and business, but many Singaporeans speak at least one other language, too. If you listen closely, you might hear a bit of "Singlish", a mix of English and all the local dialects together!

FAST FACTS

Official Name: Republic of Singapore

Capital: Singapore

Location: Southeast Asia

Official Languages: Malay, English, Mandarin Chinese, Tamil

Currency: Singapore Dollar

Population: 6 million

Area: 719 km²

Garden City

Singapore is nicknamed the "Garden City" because of its many parks and green spaces. The famous Gardens by the Bay has giant "supertrees" – tree sculptures as tall as skyscrapers, which light up at night. Even Singapore's airport houses the world's largest indoor waterfall and a lush, green butterfly garden!

Did you know?
Chewing gum was completely banned in Singapore between 1992 and 2004.

HAWKER CENTRE

Mythical Merlion

The official mascot of Singapore is the Merlion: a mythical creature with the head of a lion and the body of a fish. The fish represents Singapore's roots as a fishing village; the lion represents its old name Singapura, meaning "Lion City" in Sanskrit. The story goes that a prince looking to settle there thought he saw a lion as he came ashore, and considered it a sign of prosperity.

Food-lover's Paradise

The Malay word "*makan*? (have you eaten?)" is often used as a greeting. You can find almost any cuisine in this bustling city, often at hawker centres, which are open-air markets where you can buy lots of different types of food. Some of the most popular local foods are Hainanese chicken rice, chili crab, laksa (a spicy noodle soup), Singapore noodles, and satay (grilled meat on sticks).

REBEL GiRLS OF SiNGAPORE

Disability advocate **Theresa Goh** (b. 1987) is a Paralympic swimmer. A former breaststroke world record holder, Theresa believes in the importance of seeing ability in a person and not their disability.

Elizabeth Choy (b. 1910) secretly brought relief supplies to the prisoners of war of Singapore during World War II. After the war, she went back to teaching and became the first principal of the School of the Blind.

Arya

Family is everything to me

At school we eat Western food, but at home I mostly eat vegetarian Indian food as that's what my parents cook. *Roti prata* is a Singaporean dish with Indian influence.

I love athletic wear, although I wear dresses for special occasions, or a traditional Indian *lehenga* for cultural events. My favourite Indian celebration is the Holi festival. People throw coloured powder around to celebrate spring, the harvest, new life, and the triumph of good over evil.

Leadership Club is a committee I'm on at school. We are all fifth-graders who have been chosen to give feedback to the school on ways to improve. Some other kids in the club convinced the school to add shower curtains to the bathrooms.

I love to sing, act, and play the guitar. I often make up dance medleys with my friends to perform for our families. Otherwise, we like playing board games or badminton.

Watering the plants every day is my responsibility. We're growing herbs, lemons, and chilli plants at the moment. I also babysit my little brother; he is my only pet!

Helping people with dementia is what I'm passionate about. I have a grandpa who has it, and I see how difficult it is for the whole family. I visit him often and play memory games and music with him. I feel happiest when I am with my grandparents. My grandmother, Nani, inspires me because she is kind, talented, and smart, just like my mum.

I am in an Investors Club after school, and I want to be in finance when I'm older. I love learning about new companies and how they work.

SINGAPORE

Age: **11**

My home:
I live with my mum, dad, and little brother, Bali (8). We speak English at home. I have my own room, but I don't mind sharing when we have guests. My room is pink, absolutely everywhere you look!

My city:
Singapore is a clean and safe city to live in. It has lots of tall, shiny, modern buildings, shops, and restaurants, all surrounded by water and green spaces. We have excellent public transport and plenty of attractions, including an enormous zoo and the world's largest glasshouse.

"I would love to know what other girls want to change in the world and what inspires them."

South Korea

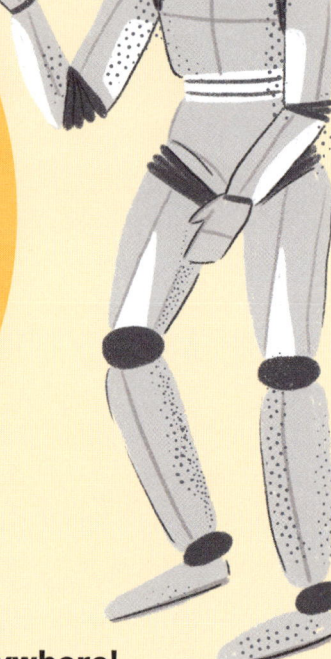

South Korea sits on the Korean Peninsula, separated from North Korea by a Demilitarized Zone (DMZ) – a region in which the armies of the two countries have agreed not to operate. The two countries separated after the Korean war, a cold-war conflict which divided the peninsula into the communist north, allied with Russia, and the capitalist south, allied with the USA. South Korea is now one of the world's leading economies, producing extremely high-tech goods and cars, and exporting globally beloved music, movies and TV.

Parks and Palaces

South Korea has some incredible places to explore. Gyeongbokgung Palace in Seoul was the first royal palace of the Joseon dynasty. Amazing city parks, like Namsan Park, are a popular place to walk, play, and enjoy nature while looking at the Seoul city skyline. Dadohaehaesang National Park offers walking trails with views of the sparkling green sea.

Technology, Everywhere!

South Korea is one of the global leaders in technology and has the world's fastest internet speeds. South Korea's government invests heavily in research and development, especially in the areas of artificial intelligence and robotics, including humanoid robots. The education system here has a strong focus on science, technology, engineering, and mathematics (STEM) subjects, which drives its exceptional progress.

FAST FACTS

Official Name: Republic of Korea

Capital: Seoul

Location: East Asia

Official Languages: Korean, South Korean Sign Language

Currency: South Korean Won

Border Country: North Korea

Population: 51.7 million

Area: 99,720 km²

SEOUL

Festivals and Traditions

South Korea has many exciting festivals, like Seollal (Lunar New Year) and Chuseok (Korean Thanksgiving). During these celebrations, families wear colourful traditional clothes called *hanbok*. They also play fun games, eat special foods, and honour their ancestors.

Did you know? Seoul-based rapper Psy's song "Gangnam Style" was the first video to be viewed one billion times on YouTube!

School Days

In South Korea, children typically go to school six days a week. They study hard, and school days are long, often lasting until late afternoon. Many children attend extra classes in important subjects, such as maths or English. South Korea's national college entrance exam, known as the Suneung, is notoriously difficult. It is an eight-hour test that determines university admission, and students study extremely hard for it.

Hallyu

The *hallyu*, or Korean Wave, refers to the global phenomenon of South Korean pop culture, including music (K-pop), dramas, fashion, and films, gaining immense popularity. K-pop groups like BTS and BLACKPINK, and Korean fashion and beauty trends have been boosted by social media where fans have instant access to Korean content. Music is a big part of Korean culture. The capital, Seoul, has an incredible number of *noraebangs* (karaoke rooms) – one for every 333 people!

Delicious Food

Kimchi, a spicy fermented vegetable dish, is eaten with almost every meal in South Korea. Other popular foods include *bulgogi* (grilled beef), *bibimbap* (a rice dish with vegetables), and *tteokbokki* (spicy rice cakes). Street food is readily available in the busy cities, and you can find tasty snacks like *hotteok* (sweet pancakes) and fishcakes at market stalls.

REBEL GIRLS OF SOUTH KOREA

Queen Seondeok of Silla (b. 606 CE) ruled the Kingdom of Silla starting in 632; the first time a woman monarch rose to power in Korean history.

K-pop band **BLACKPINK** debuted their single album *Square One* in August 2016, featuring "Whistle" and "Boombayah", their first number-one entries on South Korea's Circle Digital Chart and the US Billboard World Digital Songs chart.

Bitna

Competitions are exciting

Age: 9

My home:
I live with my mum, dad, and our pet dog, Thor. Our apartment building is very old and beautiful. It overlooks the Han River in a sought-after area of Seoul. My mum grew up here and I love hearing her old stories about the neighbourhood changing over the years. I have my own room with a canopy bed.

My city:
I live in a friendly neighbourhood of Seoul, the capital city of South Korea. It is a busy place with huge skyscrapers, street food markets, and amazing sites to visit like Gyeongbokgung Palace, where you can see ancient Korean buildings.

I enjoy walks with my family at the Han River Park. When the weather is nice in the spring and autumn, I ride along on my kickboard, or fly my kite in the breeze. We look at the beautiful scenery while picnicking or using the exercise equipment that's there for the public to enjoy.

Our dog Thor is a type of miniature bichon frise. He is like a ball of fluffy white candy floss – he always lifts my spirits! I help to take care of him by changing his water and his pad. We got him on Children's Day when I was in first grade.

I study very hard in class at school, but I have lots of fun with my friends during break time. My favourite subjects are maths and art. I like going to play at my friends' houses after school, or reading the *Sisters at War* comics.

My goal is to represent Korea as a rhythmic gymnast. I have been a registered athlete since last year, taking part in competitions. I love the excitement in the arena and the sense of accomplishment after a routine. We train hard with hoops, balls, clubs, and ribbons, and we practise high throws and rolling. I also do a lot of stretching and strength training.

New Year's Day is a special time in South Korea. We bow to our elders for pocket money and eat *tteokguk*, a traditional Lunar New Year soup that we drink to bring luck for the year ahead. It is made with thinly sliced rice cakes simmered in a clear, flavoursome beef and vegetable broth.

I like decorating my diary. My friends and I all add to it with stickers, drawings, inspirational quotes, and, of course: lots of pictures of Thor!

REBEL GIRL SUPERPOWER: ALWAYS THINKING POSITIVELY

"I'm proud when I master a new rhythmic gymnastics technique."

Sri Lanka

This island nation is sometimes referred to as "the pearl of the Indian Ocean" because of its natural beauty. Despite being a small island, Sri Lanka's wildlife is incredibly diverse. It is home to hundreds of species of animal, from the slender loris to the Sri Lankan elephant. The country is known for its iconic Raksha masks, which ward off evil with their immense eyes. Many Sri Lankan people have a love of volleyball, the national sport since 1991. Sri Lanka grows and exports tea leaves and up to 90 per cent of the world's cinnamon!

Did you know? Shaking your head means "yes" in Sri Lanka.

Precious Gems

Sri Lanka has mined gems for thousands of years. Rubies, emeralds, and even rare blue sapphires are found in places like Ratnapura, also known as the "City of Gems". Corporate mining practises can hurt the environment, so local communities and conservation groups work together to fight for better standards.

Flower Power

In Sri Lankan culture, it is customary to present fresh blooms as an offering to Buddha. Temples are covered with beautiful flowers in many colours, most commonly the sweet-scented frangipani or araliya, whose tree is familiarly known as the "temple tree". Red lotus, blue lilies, bright hibiscus, and orchids are all added to the displays. The "Queen of the Night" is a rare, fragrant, night-blooming flower that blooms only once a year and wilts before dawn.

TEA PLANTATiON

FAST FACTS

Official Name: Democratic Socialist Republic of Sri Lanka

Capital: Colombo, Sri Jayawardenepura Kotte

Location: South Asia

Official Languages: Sinhala, Tamil

Currency: Sri Lankan Rupee

Population: 22 million

Area: 65,610 km²

People and Culture

The two main groups in Sri Lanka are the Sinhalese people, who practise Buddhism and speak Sinhala, and the Tamil people, who follow Hinduism and speak Tamil. Elements of these two groups clashed in the Sri Lankan Civil War between 1983 and 2009, a conflict with roots stretching back to the British colonial period.

Holiday Hotspot

Turquoise waters, white-sand beaches and tropical sunshine make Sri Lanka a popular holiday spot for tourists. It is the world's most popular destination for nature tourism outside of Africa. Lovers of the natural world visit for elephant sanctuaries and incredible biodiversity. Sigiriya Lion Rock, an ancient rock fortress known for a massive column of rock that reaches nearly 200 metres high, is a must-see, while adventurers looking to challenge themselves can climb Adam's Peak to reach Sri Pada Temple at the summit for spectacular views.

Two Capitals

Sri Lanka has two capital cities. Sri Jayawardenepura Kotte houses the country's parliament; the port city of Colombo is the commercial capital, serving as the hub for trade, finance, and tourism. Kandy is a major city in central Sri Lanka, where you can see the famous Temple of the Sacred Tooth. Buddha's tooth is said to be preserved there, and, every summer, there's a grand festival known as Esala Perahera (Festival of the Tooth), to honour it.

Ancient Cities

Successive Sinhalese kingdoms ruled what is now Sri Lanka from 543 BCE until Britain colonized the Greater India region in 1815. Colonial rule then lasted until 1948 and left a legacy of ethnic divisions and a plantation system, both of which the country is still reckoning with today. The remains of the ancient Sinhalese capitals still stand at Anuradhapura and Polonnaruwa though, offering a powerful reminder that no systems or structures last forever.

REBEL GIRLS OF SRI LANKA

Asha de Vos (b. 1979) is a marine biologist who researches blue whales and campaigns for their protection. She is the director of a nonprofit that teaches people from all over the world why our oceans matter.

The first Sri Lankan woman to be trained as an architect, **Minnette de Silva** (b. 1918) went on to become internationally acclaimed. She is considered a pioneer of the modern architectural style in Sri Lanka.

Binuli

My family calls me Binu

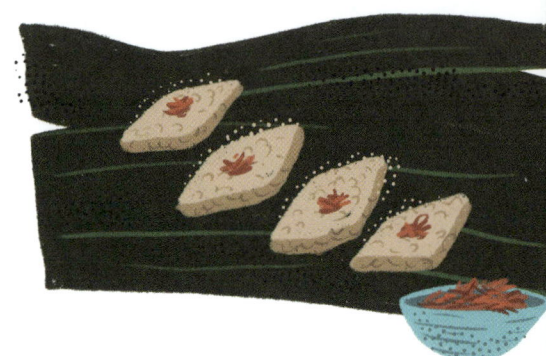

Age: 13

My home:
I live with my mother, my father, my elder sister, Janani, our two cats, and our dogs, Jimmy and Tina. I love them all dearly. We speak Sinhala at home and at school. I share my bedroom with my sister, who decorates the walls with her artwork. My favourite thing in my room is definitely my panda plushie.

My village:
I live in a beautiful village, surrounded by a vast reservoir and beautiful mountains. The landscape is dotted with lush, green paddy fields. It is a peaceful and scenic place to live. My area was once part of the second-oldest of all of Sri Lanka's kingdoms, Polonnaruwa. You can still visit The Ancient City of Polonnaruwa, which has lots of temple ruins and ancient monuments, and has been declared a UNESCO World Heritage Site.

¶ I love celebrating the New Year. In April, at the end of the annual harvest, Sri Lankans of all backgrounds come together to toast the fresh opportunities a new year brings. It's a time for wearing new clothes, visiting relatives, and enjoying festive traditions. We eat beautifully shaped sweet treats and light the hearth to boil milk for *kiribath* – rice cooked in creamy coconut milk. It symbolizes new life and good fortune. My mother makes a special version with green *gram* (mung beans). It's my absolute favourite!

¶ I'm proud of overcoming the challenges my speech impairment brings with it. My resilience, along with the love and support of my parents, teachers, and friends, gives me strength. "සහකම්පනය" ("*sahakampanaya*") is how we write "empathy" in Sinhala: the ability to understand and share in someone else's emotions, whether joy or sadness. I am lucky to have kind friends. School is a happy place for me because I get to spend time with them.

¶ I love going on sightseeing trips with my parents, taking in the beauty of my country. The Indian Ocean, which surrounds our island, is breathtaking. I also admire the Ruwanweliseya, a sacred stupa built by King Dutugemunu in 140 BCE. When my condition limits how much I can read, I look for books with beautiful illustrations of different places so I can dream of new adventures.

¶ Dancing and cycling with my friends brings me joy, even though my speech impairment sometimes makes interaction difficult and tiring because I have to find my own ways of communicating. On weekends, I mostly stay home with my parents, but sometimes we go out in nature. I love watching gymnasts perform on TV; I dream of trying the moves myself.

"I love to wear the dresses my mother stitches for me on special occasions."

අනුකම්පාව
(empathy)

EUROPE

Denmark

Did you know? There are more pigs in Denmark than humans.

Denmark is the super flat, southernmost country of the area known as Scandinavia in Northern Europe. It is made up of the Jutland Peninsula and more than 400 islands. The Kingdom of Denmark has the oldest unbroken monarchy in Europe. Its king is the ceremonial leader of mainland Denmark, Greenland, and the Faroe Islands. As one of the first countries in the world to introduce a welfare system for its people, Denmark is known for being particularly family-focused.

Islands Galore

There are people living on around 70 of Denmark's 400 islands. The largest island is Zealand, where the capital city, Copenhagen, is located. Everyone lives near the water – no part of the country is more than 67 kilometres from the North or Baltic Seas! The total area of Denmark is roughly the same size as the Netherlands or Estonia.

Viking Warriors

Between the 8th and 11th centuries, Denmark was home to the Vikings! Viking sailors, traders, and warriors from Scandinavia travelled to many parts of Europe, Asia, and North America. They built distinctive longships that helped them to navigate the seas. Today, Denmark has many museums and historic sites where you can learn about Viking history, such as the National Museum in Copenhagen and the Viking Ship Museum in Roskilde.

Environment and Renewable Energy

Denmark is a world leader in renewable energy, using its natural resources like wind and sun to make power. About 50 per cent of Denmark's electricity comes from wind energy, and the country has more than 6,000 wind turbines! Denmark has also set a goal to become carbon neutral by 2050, meaning they want to reduce their pollution to protect the planet.

FAST FACTS

Official Name: Kingdom of Denmark

Capital: Copenhagen

Location: Northern Europe, Scandinavia

Border Country: Germany

Official Language: Danish

Currency: Danish Krone

Population: 6 million

Area: 43,094 km²

COPENHAGEN

Cosy *Hygge*

Hygge (pronounced "hoo-gah") is a uniquely Danish word that means creating a warm and peaceful atmosphere. It's about enjoying simple pleasures, like sipping hot chocolate with friends, reading a good book, or lighting candles on a cold evening. Danes embrace *hygge* during the long winter months, as a way to feel connected to loved ones. It's all about making life feel cosy and joyful.

Capital City

Copenhagen is the capital city of Denmark. About a quarter of Denmark's population lives in its suburbs! The city is known for being very cycle-friendly, with more bikes than cars. One if its most famous landmarks is the *Little Mermaid* statue, based on the fairy tale by Danish author Hans Christian Andersen.

The Love of Play

Denmark places a strong emphasis on children's well-being and creativity. The country has a great balance between school and free time, allowing kids to enjoy outdoor activities and games. It is also the birthplace of the world-famous LEGO® bricks, that inspire and develop the builders of tomorrow. The name "LEGO" comes from "*leg godt*", which means "play well" in Danish.

Danish Pastries

Danish pastries are loved all over the world. They come in many different shapes, with delicious fillings, such as chocolate, jam, cinnamon sugar, or custard. In Denmark it's traditional to have a *kagemand* or *kagekone* ("cake man or woman") at your birthday party: a person-shaped cake that's meant to represent the birthday child! It is usually covered in jelly sweets and little Danish flags, and you make a wish when you cut into it.

REBEL GIRLS OF DENMARK

Queen Margrethe II (b. 1940) is the former Queen of Denmark. She reigned for 52 years until January 2024. On top of her duties as monarch, she worked as a costume designer, scenographer, and an illustrator.

Rebecca Roos Jensen (b. 2003) was the youngest Danish woman to qualify as a pilot, in 2020. Rebecca got her pilot's license at age 17, and for her, the sky is truly the limit.

Eva

I'm from the city of smiles!

Age: 10

My family:
I am an only child and my parents are separated, so I split my time between my mom and dad's houses. I have cats at both homes! Mikki is 12 years old and is big, cute, and lazy, and Kittemau is smaller and is only 6! I love the pink walls and light-up Hollywood mirror that I have in my bedroom at Mom's house.

My city:
Aarhus is known as "the city of smiles". It's an historic city on the east coast of Denmark with an iconic harbour and beautiful forests nearby. We have a rainbow sculpture on top of the art museum that you can walk inside!

My suburb is known for its focus on sustainability and community living. We see our neighbours a lot, and we share one giant trampoline between all the children. I always ride my bike wherever possible to protect the environment.

Gymnastics is my passion. I absolutely love it! I attend the small club at my school and love to watch it on TV, too. I also play paddle tennis in my spare time.

A traditional Danish dish that I enjoy is toasted rye bread. I eat it with butter and canned mackerel. "*Rødgrød med fløde*" is both a traditional Danish dessert and a tongue-twister that foreigners often can't say. It's a pudding made with cooked red berries sweetened with sugar, served with double cream or delicious ice cream.

I love to read fantasy stories full of magic and adventure, like *Impossible Creatures* and the *Harry Potter* books. Hermione Granger is my favourite character.

I enjoy being creative with my friends. We film short, funny movies and edit them with CapCut (video-editing software). We love to make up dances together, too. I think I would like to be a TV presenter or an actor when I'm older. I'm inspired by Stephania Potalivo, who is on Danish TV.

I cook dinner every Monday night. I also take the rubbish out for recycling and help by setting the table for meals and clearing up afterwards.

"*I always try to be a good friend, which I think is the most important thing you can be.*"

Finland

As one of the northernmost countries on the planet, Finland receives nearly 24 hours of sunlight a day during summer. Its winters are long, with temperatures often below freezing, and snow covering much of the country. This flat land of lakes, forests, and folklore has been ranked #1 in the UN's "World Happiness Report" on global wellness every year between 2016–2024. Finland's capital, Helsinki, is famous for its design and architecture, as well as unique sauna locations such as the Allas Sea Pools.

Did you know? Finland hosts the annual Air Guitar World Championships each year, in Oulu.

Fun in the Forest

Forests cover almost 75 per cent of the country, and many Finnish people enjoy spending time in nature – whether picking fruit such as lingonberries, bilberries, or cloudberries, or simply taking a peaceful walk. They just need to watch out for bears and wolves! Finland's more than 188,000 lakes are great places for outdoor activities like fishing, canoeing, and swimming.

Elves and Spirits

In Finnish folklore, elves and forest spirits are magical beings called *haltijas* or *tonttus* that help people, protect homes, and bring good luck. *Haltijas* are sprite-like and can be found outdoors, whereas *tonttus* are home elves, often described as small, elderly men who help with chores. *Saunatonttu* are elves who are said to live in the walls of Finnish saunas, keeping everyone safe!

FAST FACTS

Capital: Helsinki

Official Name: Republic of Finland

Location: Northern Europe, Scandinavia

Border Countries: Norway, Russia, Sweden

Official Languages: Finnish, Swedish

Currency: Euro

Population: 5.6 million

Area: 338,143 km²

Education in Finland

The Finnish education system is often ranked one of the best in the world. Education is free for children, who start their schooling at age seven. In the early years, Finnish school includes lots of play time and outdoor activities no matter the weather — all year round! Teachers are highly trained and respected.

Leader in Gender Equality

Finland was the first country in Europe to grant women the right to vote and stand for election; Finnish women have been able to do both since 1906. Finland was also the first country to elect women to its parliament. In 2003, Finland made history when both its president and prime minister were women, the first time that had happened in Europe.

Hot and Cold

The sauna — a small room heated with steam — plays a special part in Finnish culture. Nearly every Finnish home has one, and there are more than three million of them across the country! People use saunas to relax, get clean, and enjoy quiet time. After sweating in the hot steam, many people take a quick dip in a lake or roll in the snow to cool off.

Arctic Lapland

Sitting above the Arctic Circle, Lapland is a vast ecosystem of fells, tundra, forests, and lakes. It is home to the Sámi people, who are indigenous to the northern parts of Norway, Sweden, Finland, and Russia. Snow and ice blanket the region from November until late May. It has more reindeer than people — 200,000 of them!

REBEL GiRLS OF FiNLAND

Liina Heikkinen (b. 2007), gained artistic recognition at the Young Wildlife Photographer of the Year 2020, when she submitted her photo of a fox fiercely defending the remains of a barnacle goose from its rivals.

Johanna Nordblad (b. 1975) is a fearless Finnish designer, ice diver, and freediver. As a freediver, she has set both national and global records.

Stella

Bright colours make me happy!

I attend a bilingual school, where we speak both Finnish and English. We also have to learn Swedish as it is the second national language in Finland. We speak Finnish, German, and English at home. I am proud of my language skills!

School starts between 8:30am and 10:15am. It's later on Mondays because my teachers say we need more rest after the weekend! It is mandatory to go outdoors during break, no matter the weather. Lunch is at 11:30am, followed by another 30-minute break. School continues until 1:30pm or 3:15pm if we started later. We often have weeks when we decide ourselves what we learn and when – I like it a lot.

I dance four times a week, and I am proud of my first competition medal. My dance styles are disco (not from the 70s!), show, and ballet. I want to be a performer when I'm older. Dancing and listening to music make me so happy. I also like athletics and enjoy watching women's ice hockey.

Laskiainen is a very special Finnish festival. At the end of winter, just before Lent, we all have the day off school or work to make the most of all the snow, going sledging or skiing with friends. We eat sweet buns filled with whipped cream and jam. They are delicious!

I go to a weekly art class, and am proud of my creativity. I love making my ideas a reality through paint or craft.

I like comfortable clothes that I can move easily in, whether it's climbing during recess, or jumping on the trampoline with friends. I like colourful prints and outfits. My winter clothes need to be bright since Finnish winter days are dark and long.

Age: 12

My home:
I live with my mom, my dad, and our little black dog, Omppu (it means "small apple" in Finnish). He is one of the family and we love him so much. I have my own room. It is decorated with a Pokémon clock, a Vincent Van Gogh picture (not an original!), and a picture that says "DISCO", which I got in London. I have various books, LEGO® sets, and many bright, colourful things.

My city:
Espoo is a very green city to the west of Helsinki. I like that I can walk or ride my bike to most places, including school and the shops. We also have beautiful forests and regularly spend time there at the weekend.

REBEL GIRL SUPERPOWER: MY ABILITY TO INSPIRE OTHERS

France

Culture Vultures
Art, literature, and film are an important part of French culture. France has produced many famous artists, such as the 19th-century Impressionists Claude Monet and Berthe Morisot. The Louvre in Paris is the most visited art gallery in the world.

Officially named the French Republic, France is the largest country in Western Europe. It is also known as "l'Hexagone" ("the Hexagon") because of its resemblance on a map to the six-sided shape, but it actually shares its borders with no fewer than eight countries! From snowy peaks in the Alps to the glamorous beach resorts of the French Riviera, it is one of the most visited countries in Europe. It is famous for its culture, gourmet food, and fashion – and the revolutionary spirit that led it to become Europe's first republic in 1792.

The Eiffel Tower, Paris, is repainted every 7 years.

ANTiBES | FRENCH RiViERA

FAST FACTS

Official Name: French Republic

Capital: Paris

Location: Europe

Border Countries: Andorra, Belgium, Germany, Italy, Luxembourg, Monaco, Spain, Switzerland

Official Language: French

Currency: Euro

Population: 68.5 million

Area: 551,500 km²

Fashion Capital
Paris's label as the "fashion capital of the world" dates as far back as the 17th century, when King Louis XIV began encouraging his court to copy his flamboyant style. Today, Paris is home to many of the world's most iconic fashion houses, including Chanel, Christian Dior, and Louis Vuitton. Paris Fashion Week is a huge event. Designers, journalists, and celebrities travel from all over for a first look at the next big thing in style.

School Life

Did you know most French schools are closed on Wednesdays – either for the whole day, or just the afternoon? This is when French school kids catch up on their extracurricular activities, homework, or simply rest! School is free and compulsory from the ages of six to 16 in France, with many children staying until they are 18.

FRENCH ALPS

Awesome Alps

The highest peak in Western Europe, Mont Blanc ("white mountain"), is found in France. A mighty 4,807 metres high at its peak, Mont Blanc is part of a vast mountain range system called the Alps, that stretches into 10 other European countries beyond France. The French Alps is home to a thriving variety of wildlife, including lynx, wolves, wild boar, and golden eagles. It is also a popular destination for skiers and snowboarders.

Language of Love

French is the sixth most spoken language in the world after English, Chinese, Hindi, Spanish, and Arabic, and is an official language in 29 countries, including Haiti and Madagascar, due to France's colonial history. Even if you don't speak French, you might know some phrases from cooking, or from ballet, where it is traditionally used to describe techniques and actions.

Did you know? It is considered bad luck in France to place a baguette face down on a table, or a hunger curse may befall you or anyone who eats it!

Food Glorious Food

Cheese, wine, croissants... French produce is world-renowned. France's most famous style of cooking, *haute cuisine*, is known for its impeccable presentation. So is its *patisserie*: beautifully crafted pastries that look too good to eat! But it's not all fancy fare; *goûter* is the French custom of having a sweet snack after school. Often it's just a simple piece of chocolate folded into a baguette, then dipped in a bowl of hot chocolate!

REBEL GIRLS OF FRANCE

Josephine Baker (b. 1906) was an American-born French entertainer, civil rights activist, and member of the French Resistance during World War II. She used her fame to fight for racial equality.

Katia Krafft (b. 1942) was a French volcanologist. She was fascinated with the beauty and fury of volcanoes right from her childhood. She died tragically while filming an eruption at Mount Unzen, Japan.

PARIS | FRANCE

Age: 8

My family:
I live with my mum and my sister, Simone (6), in a small fifth-floor apartment. I love to watch the planes, sunsets, and twinkling city lights from the bedroom window I share with my little sister. Our building has a small park outside it where I meet my friends. It's near the Canal Saint-Martin.

My city:
Paris is the French capital. It was built on the banks of the River Seine. It is known as "the City of Lights" and is famous for the Eiffel Tower, which lights up at night. The Louvre is a world-renowned art gallery where you can see lots of famous paintings, like Leonardo da Vinci's *Mona Lisa*.

Rita

My nickname is Ritatouille!

I love walking in the city. I especially like going out with my mum at weekends, hunting for hidden street art. An artist called "Invader" has been secretly painting little mosaic-style pictures all over Paris for the past 20 years. I love spotting new ones and taking photos of them.

Dancing is my favourite hobby. I attend classic dance classes twice a week, and I also do hip-hop dance classes at school. I'm having double bass lessons and I like learning to play an instrument, but practising takes a lot of work.

I ride my bike to my dance class, and I love to rollerblade in the parks near my apartment. Sometimes I take the Metro but I don't like it very much.

I don't like wearing constricting outfits. I much prefer to feel comfortable, so I like wearing crop tops with baggy trousers. I often wear black.

Our family traditions make me happy. My mum, sister, and I start the day with a family hug before we get ready for school. We call it *"le câlin du matin"* ("the morning cuddle"!). We also have a little dance party every Friday evening, with *aperitivi* (little snacks) and drinks. It's my job to be the DJ!

I'm passionate about reading. I love *Harry Potter* and Greek mythology, and I like Roald Dahl's books. I enjoy French comic books, too, like *The Legendaries*.

Sleepovers with my friends are so fun. We dress up, watch movies, and sometimes put on mini musicals!

Germany

Surrounded by nine neighbours in the centre of Europe, and bordered at the top by the North Sea and the Baltic Sea, lies Germany. Around 30 per cent of its land is covered with dense forests. The Bavarian Alps to the south offer stunning views, and major rivers, such as the Rhine and the Danube, cut through the land. Being one of the most populated countries in Europe, it has lively cities that people flock to visit, including the ultra-cool capital city of Berlin, known for its art, music, museums, and festivals.

Oktoberfest

Munich plays host to Oktoberfest every autumn: a huge festival in which people eat, drink, and enjoy rides at a fair. It is so much fun that it is recreated in many cities around the world. Foods loved by festivalgoers include sausages, such as *bratwurst*, which are usually made from pork, and *pretzels*, a type of bread that is tied into a knot before it is baked.

Did you know?
Germany started the tradition of decorating Christmas trees, way back in the 16th century.

FAST FACTS

Official Name: Federal Republic of Germany

Capital: Berlin

Location: Europe

Border Countries: Austria, Belgium, Czechia, Denmark, France, Luxembourg, the Netherlands, Poland, Switzerland

Official Language: German

Currency: Euro

Population: 83.5 million

Area: 357,022 km²

Nuremberg Castle

Constructed in the Middles Ages, Nuremberg Castle is a medieval fortress that looms over its surroundings. It is paired with a stretch of walls that encircles the oldest parts of the city, built as a defence. Germany once had a royal family, and during that time this was a palace used by monarchs. You can still climb one of its towers today, and check out its 50-metre-deep well.

Creating Cars

For hundreds of years, car manufacturing has been an important part of Germany's economy. Mercedes-Benz is one example of a company that was started here. One of its founders, Karl Benz, took out a patent for the first ever petrol-powered car. Today, the country is working on getting more cars on to the road that use renewable energy.

Culture Capital

The capital city of Berlin is buzzing with different cultural experiences. There are several UNESCO World Heritage sites to explore, including Peacock Island, as well as quirkier places such as the Lipstick Museum. It is also the only city in the world with three opera houses. Looking down on it all is the tallest structure in Germany, the Fernsehturm, a tower built to transmit TV and radio signals that now has a revolving restaurant at the top!

THE BLACK FOREST

Street Art Central

Germany is a welcoming place for street artists, who create their work on urban buildings and walls. In Cologne, the Ehrenfeld district has awe-inspiring street art on every corner, and the city of Munich has produced an official Street Art Map to help people find their favourite pieces. MadC, a German artist, is famous for her epic 700-square-metre "700-Wall" mural on the railway line between Berlin and Halle. It is thought to be the largest mural made by a single person.

The Black Forest

Rich with nature and impressive scenery, the mountainous Black Forest region blankets southwestern Germany with oak, beech, and fir woodlands. It is a wonderful place to spot wildlife, including dormice, boar, pine martens, and wood grouse. This area is also famous for its handmade cuckoo clocks, and its black forest gateau – layers of chocolate sponge with cherries and cream.

REBEL GIRLS OF GERMANY

Emilie Snethlage (b. 1868) dedicated her life to studying Brazilian birds. A German-born Brazilian naturalist and ornithologist, she made significant contributions to the understanding of the Amazon's birdlife.

In 1982, at the age of 13, **Steffi Graf** (b. 1969) played her first professional tennis match, making her the youngest phenom to turn professional. She lost, but that didn't discourage her – she would soon be a world number one.

Lisa

Swimming makes me happy!

I was diagnosed with scoliosis a year ago. It's a spine condition that affects my posture. Now, I wear a back brace and do special exercises to make me stronger. I am getting better every day. My back brace has palm trees on it. I like the colour, but I sometimes choose baggy clothes to hide it. My mum founded a support group, "Skoliosekids". It helps to talk to other girls going through the same thing.

School starts at 8am and we finish at 1pm, which might seem early, but in Germany we go to a type of after-school club called *Mittagsbetreuung*. We call it "Mitti". We eat with the other pupils and do our homework. After that, we have time to play, either indoors or outdoors. We can play table football or do arts and crafts.

I love to read detective stories, I find them so exciting! I try to solve the cases as I read along. Reading helps me to feel calm; I read a book a week. I also enjoy crafting and painting with my friends.

My brother and I help out at home. We each have to choose one thing per week, like doing the dishes or taking the bins out. I like doing it.

Munich is a very bike-friendly city. I cycle to school every day and get around by bike at weekends. For longer journeys I take the train.

Exercise is so important for my back; I do something nearly every day. Sport is a big part of my life, especially swimming. I love going to my weekly swimming club, and to the climbing wall. I also enjoy rollerblading and am learning parkour (jumping and climbing over buildings and objects).

Age: 9

My home:
I live with my mum, my dad, and my little brother, Julian (6). I have my own bedroom. I painted my bed turquoise and I have a light-blue canopy over it, and fairy lights. My curtains are rainbow-coloured and I have lots of photos of family and friends on the walls.

My city:
Munich is a large city in the south of Germany. It is famous for Oktoberfest. People travel from all over the world to attend it. They wear traditional outfits: *lederhosen* for men, and *dirndl* for women.

Age: 8

My home:
I live with my mum and dad. I am an only child and I have my own room. It is filled with paint-by-numbers pictures I have painted myself, and so many cuddly toys. I love them!

My city:
Berlin is the capital of Germany. Its most famous landmarks are the Brandenburg Gate and the wall that divided the city in two until 1989, but you can't really see it anymore. We live on the outskirts, on a cosy street with playgrounds and a big forest right behind our house.

Thea

My family calls me TeTe

There is a lot of traffic in Berlin, and there is garbage on the street in some places. My mum sometimes drives me to school in the car, but I also ride my bike, walk, or take the bus. Preventing too much pollution is important to me because I want to save the rainforests.

My school day starts at 8am and ends at 12:30pm, when we go to after-school care. Even though I sometimes find school exhausting, I often play school with my friends when we meet up. That way we can be the teachers for the day!

Painting makes me very happy. I really enjoy it, and I'm proud that I can paint well. My favourite thing to paint is clothes. Sometimes I even add painted illustrations to my stories.

"Little puppies make me the happiest! I would love to run a dog kennel when I'm older."

Christmas is my favourite time! An elf comes to our house during Advent and I unwrap a present from a special calendar every day until Christmas Eve, when we have our main Christmas celebration in Germany. My family comes round in the afternoon to eat cake, then we go to church to sing carols before returning to open presents and eat dinner. We usually have sausages and lots of different salads.

I have five pet snails. I collected them outside our house. Their names are Emily, Marilyn, Fipsi, Kermit, and Mia. They love eating cucumbers and they lay lots of eggs. I love animals and desperately want a pet dog!

I go horse riding in my spare time. I want to become a famous dressage rider one day. I also do athletics, and I play the piano.

Greece

Blue and White
Splashed across Greece are the iconic colours of blue and white: a colour pairing that Greeks have identified with for centuries. These are the colours of the nation's flag, and on the beautiful island of Santorini, many of the houses are whitewashed, with blue doors and window frames. While very striking to look at, whitewash does also have a practical purpose. It helps to keep the buildings cool by reflecting the rays of the sun.

Sun-kissed Greece has the longest coastline of all the countries on the Mediterranean. It has a sea-faring heritage stretching all the way back to ancient times, and shipping is one of its biggest industries. The bustling port in the capital, Athens, handles cruise ships, passenger boats, and gigantic vessels transporting goods around the world. Athens also boasts the Acropolis, an ancient citidel. As well as its sizeable mainland, Greece is made up of 6,000 islands, although people live on only 227 of them.

FAST FACTS

Official Name: Hellenic Republic

Capital: Athens

Location: Southeast Europe

Official Language: Greek

Border Countries: Albania, Bulgaria, North Macedonia, Türkiye

Currency: Euro

Population: 10.4 million

Area: 131,957 km²

All About Olives
For more than 6,000 years, olives and olive trees have been an integral part of Greek life. In the ancient Olympic Games, winners were given wreaths made from olive branches, rather than gold medals. Greece is one of the world's biggest producers of olives, which are actually a type of fruit. The kalamata olive, with its beautiful purple skin and meaty texture, is a particularly delicious variety.

THE ACROPOLIS

Going for Gold
The ancient Olympic Games were founded in Olympia, Greece, in 776 BCE. It was an enormously popular event with ancient Greeks. Alongside long jump, boxing, and javelin, there was also chariot racing. And, athletes competed completely naked! Those ancient games were stopped during the Roman Empire in around 393 CE. In 1896, the games were revived, and the first modern Olympic Games were held in Athens.

Big Thinking
Thousands of years ago, the ancient Greeks contributed to the development of modern disciplines like theatre and mathematics. Big-thinking philosophers, such as Plato, and his pupil, Aristotle, proposed a way of thinking about ethics and logic that in turn helped to shape modern thinking on these topics in Western Europe. Plato is also thought to have invented the alarm clock to make sure his pupils got to class on time!

Did you know?
Athens is named after a goddess, Athena, worshipped by ancient Greeks.

Marine Parks
Greece has a number of marine parks to protect the rich wildlife found in the Mediterranean Sea. Some fascinating creatures are being protected in these zones, such as dolphins, the loggerhead sea turtle, and the Mediterranean monk seal. There are also unique habitats here, including knobbly coral reefs, as well as meadows of *Posidonia*, a type of seagrass that is only found in these waters.

REBEL GIRLS OF GREECE

Maria Callas (b. 1923) was born in America to Greek parents. When she moved to Greece as a teenager, she began singing, and became one of the greatest opera singers the world has ever seen.

Hypatia (b. c. 350 CE) studied in the great library of the ancient Egyptian city of Alexandria and grew up to teach astronomy, maths, and philosophy. She invented the astrolabe, a tool for measuring the positions of stars.

A Mythical Mountain
The many gods and goddesses worshipped by the ancient Greeks lived on Mount Olympus. But this mountain is not just in the myths – it is a real place, still standing as tall as it did thousands of years ago. The highest mountain in Greece, its fog-laden peak is such a majestic sight that it is no wonder it was a special place for early Greeks.

Myrsini

I want to dance professionally

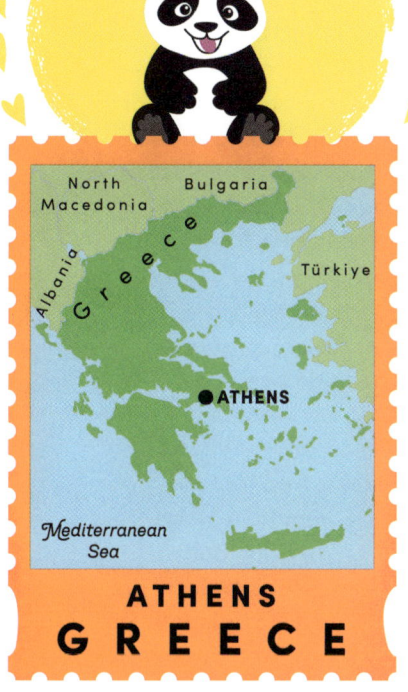

ATHENS GREECE

I usually eat cereal for breakfast. For lunch and dinner, I eat home-cooked food. My favourite Greek food is *pastitsio*, a thick pasta with minced meat and béchamel sauce on top. Some people also add breadcrumbs.

On a typical school day I get up at 7am. My dad drives me and my sister to school, where we do our lessons and have three breaks during the day. At school we speak Greek, English, and German. I return home at 3pm on the school bus, and do my homework, practise dancing, play the drums, and do my extracurricular maths and reading.

My favourite hobby of all is hip-hop dancing. I attend classes twice per week. My dance team won a gold medal in a competition recently. That made me really proud.

I love Christmas! It's my favourite time of the year – not just because it's my birthday, but because very occasionally it snows in Athens and I love to make igloos with my mum. We also like to make special Greek Christmas sweets, called *melomakarona* with honey and walnuts, and *kourabiedes*, with caster sugar and almonds.

I love my friends. When we are together we talk, we eat, we run through the school, we play hide-and-seek, and we walk hand-in-hand.

My favourite sport to watch is rhythmic gymnastics. I also love reading. I prefer action adventure books.

Age: 8

My home:
I live with my parents, my sister, Smaragda (meaning "emerald", 6), my sister, Melina (4), and my fluffy white dog, Booky. My room is big and bright, with lots of stickers on the walls. My books and my fluffy stuffed panda bear are my favourite things in it.

My city:
I live in Athens, the capital of Greece. It is a beautiful city, famous for its ancient history and for being the first known democracy in the world. The Parthenon still stands in Athens; it is the symbol of ancient Greece.

REBEL GIRL SUPERPOWER: KNOWING HOW TO DO CARTWHEELS

Ireland

Tech Hub
Ireland is known as the tech hub of Europe, with many of the world's biggest tech firms choosing to locate their European HQ in the country. The capital, Dublin, is a hive of new ideas, with Google and Facebook just some of the huge companies rubbing shoulders in the city. Away from Dublin, Apple's European HQ can be found in Cork, and Limerick and Galway are also thriving hotspots. Feeding this tech boom is Ireland's young, talented STEM workforce. In 2022, Ireland had the highest number of STEM graduates for every 1000 people aged 20–29 in Europe.

Ireland is known as "the Emerald Isle", thanks to regular rain that keeps its grasslands green! Rugged cliffs and cobbled cities form the backdrop to a tradition of storytelling through music, dance, and literature. After centuries of colonial rule by England and opposition to that rule, the island was partitioned in 1921. This happened because some people wanted Irish independence but others didn't. The Republic of Ireland (*Éire* in Irish) is 80 per cent of the island, while the rest, Northern Ireland has remained part of the UK.

Did you know? Ireland's harp is the only national symbol of a country that is a musical instrument.

SKELLIG MICHAEL

Rugged Beauty
From the Cliffs of Moher to Killarney National Park, Ireland is full of natural beauty. Spot animals like red deer, otters, and even puffins, who breed in their thousands on the beautiful island of Skellig Michael (*Sceilg Mhichíl*). Ireland was completely covered by thick glaciers 15,000 years ago. These giant shifting sheets of ice stripped the soil, leaving huge flat limestone rocks. The Burren, the rocky area on the west coast of Ireland, is evidence of this today.

FAST FACTS

Official Name: Republic of Ireland (*Éire*)

Capital: Dublin

Location: Europe

Official Language: Irish (*Gaeilge*), English

Currency: Euro

Population: 5.38 million

Area: 70,273 km^2

Traditions

Traditional folk music and dance have been passed down through generations. Fiddles, flutes, the Irish harp, and the *bodhrán* (an Irish drum) liven up any celebration. The fast footwork and energetic rhythms of Irish dancing are incredible to watch – and dancers perform without moving their upper body! Many Irish people still embrace their ancient sporting traditions, too. Sports including Gaelic football, Gaelic handball, hurling, and rounders, are played widely.

Going Green!

Saint Patrick's Day is an annual celebration of all things Irish. What started as a religious festival honouring the patron saint of Ireland has become a wider celebration of Irish culture through music, dance, parades, and, of course – wearing green! Shamrocks are worn on 17 March because Saint Patrick is said to have used a shamrock's three leaves to explain the Holy Trinity when he brought Christianity to Ireland.

Capital City

The capital city of Dublin is packed with beautiful green spaces, including the National Botanic Gardens, which is home to six plant species now extinct in the wild. Dublin is also home to the 1,200-year-old Book of Kells, which is described as "Ireland's greatest treasure". The illustrated medieval manuscript is in remarkable condition, with its colours still vivid today, and with hand-drawn detail so intricate some of it can't be seen by the naked eye!

Children's Books

Authors and illustrators of books for children can thrive in Ireland – and young readers can too! The organization Children's Books Ireland supports artists and authors by arranging book awards, conferences, and grants to pay for things like rent and food. Recipients of the Tyrone Guthrie Centre bursary are awarded a stay on a peaceful country estate where they get time and space to focus on creating their books. Children's Books Ireland also run book "clinics", where young readers can chat to "Book Doctors". Each child leaves with a "prescription" to take to the library or bookshop, for their perfect read!

REBEL GiRLS OF IRELAND

Anne Bonny (b. 1697) was a pirate who served under John Rackham. One of the few recorded female pirates in the Golden Age of Piracy, she has become one of the most recognized pirates of the era.

In June 2024, **Sarah Friar** (b. 1972) joined OpenAI, the artificial intelligence research organization that develops ChatGPT, as its first CFO. Now Sarah pioneers the future of artificial intelligence and how to embrace it.

Naomi

I'm happiest when drawing

Age: 9

My home:
I live with my mum, my dad, my sister, Alannah (12), and my brother, Cian (6). I share a room with Alannah. We have bunk beds and I sleep at the top. We have posters on the walls of Taylor Swift, Olivia Rodrigo, and Hatsune Miku.

My town:
Leixlip is a town in County Kildare where the River Rye and the River Liffey meet. Its Irish name is Léim an Bhradáin ("the salmon leap"). We have some shops, two churches, and a farmer's market on Saturdays. There is a lot of wildlife. I have seen foxes, badgers, rabbits, hedgehogs, deer, and even a barn owl! There are a lot of sports clubs including soccer, Gaelic games, rugby, and tennis.

I usually eat eggs on toast for breakfast. For lunch, I might have a smoothie, popcorn, cucumber, or sushi. For dinner, we have spaghetti bolognese, roast chicken, or sausages and mash. Dad makes really good Irish soda bread. It's lovely with homemade soup that Mum makes.

We start our school day with reading or drawing. Then we have *obair na maidine* ("morning work" in Irish), which is maths or handwriting practice, before our *lón beag* ("little lunch"). We go to the yard and I play with my friends or read. Next, we learn Irish, English, and then break for *lón mór* ("big lunch"). We get a 30-minute break. Some people play football or tag; I usually read or draw.

I want to be an animator. I love anime and I am really passionate about art and computers. I am happiest when I am drawing and I love reading graphic novels, manga, and murder mysteries. I am currently reading *Murder Most Unladylike* by Robin Stevens.

There is a TV show here called *The Late Late Show*. It's on every Friday night in Ireland. Once a year, they have *The Late Late Toy Show* instead. It showcases all the new toys that are coming for Christmas. We get to stay up late to watch it, eat treats, and hang out. I love it!

My friends and I bring little teddies to the end of the green. We sit under the trees and pretend to be different characters. We go out riding on our bikes and we play on the trampoline, too.

I have joined the chess club at school. I'm also part of the guitar club and I do gymnastics every week.

"I'm inspired by Taylor Swift and Mum. Taylor's an amazing singer and Mum is an amazing woman."

Italy

The nation of Italy juts out into the surrounding water of Southern Europe in the shape of a heeled boot. The islands of Sicily and Sardinia lie off the west coast, with white, sandy beaches and warm sunshine. The north is dominated by the Alps, a snowy mountain range that sweeps across Italy and its bordering countries. Its capital, Rome, is full of ruins of the ancient, powerful Roman empire that existed for around 12 centuries. Rome also includes Vatican City, one of the world's smallest countries and home of the Catholic Church.

Incredible Buildings

Italian architecture is a feast for the eyes. The Leaning Tower of Pisa is a bell tower that is famous for standing at a slant. The Duomo in Florence is a domed cathedral with stunning views over the city. And the ancient Colosseum in Rome is a vast structure in which thousands would watch gruesome spectacles like cruel gladiator fights to the death, or brutal re-enactments of naval battles, complete with ships and water.

Fast Cars

Italy is renowned for its racing car heritage. Italian brands Ferrari, Lamborghini, and Maserati are known for their speed and style. Lamborghini cars have sharp, bold shapes, while bright red Ferrari cars zoom around tracks at incredible speeds. The Autodromo Nazionale Monza near Milan is one of the fastest tracks in the world, and is home to the Formula One Italian Grand Prix.

FAST FACTS

Official Name: Italian Republic

Capital: Rome

Location: Southern and Western Europe

Border Countries: Austria, France, Slovenia, Switzerland

Official Language: Italian

Currency: Euro

Population: 59 million

Area: 301,340 km^2

The Renaissance

Italy is particularly known for a period of amazing artistic output known as the Renaissance in the 14th, 15th, and 16th centuries. This was a creative age, and artists were inspired by the ancient civilizations that had come before them. Famous artists of this era include Leonardo da Vinci and Raphael Sanzio da Urbino, as well as Sofonisba Anguissola and Artemisia Gentileschi.

VENiCE

Did you know?

The city of Venice is spread across 118 islands, connected by more than 400 bridges. It is known as "the Floating City".

Preserved Pompeii

Bubbling volcanoes pepper the landscape of Italy. Mount Etna in Sicily is Europe's tallest volcano, at around 3,300 metres high. But another, Mount Vesuvius, is historically important. In 79 CE, Vesuvius erupted and buried the nearby city of Pompeii in ash and rock. When Pompeii was excavated in the 1700s, a well-preserved city was revealed, frozen at the very moment it was destroyed.

Buon Appetito!

A true feast awaits you in Italy! Mouthwatering pizza was first sold under that name in Naples in the 1500s. Pasta, which today is eaten in households around the world, is the country's pride and joy. Each region has its own varieties, meaning that there are thousands of different types. For dessert, try a scoop (or two) of gelato, a rich frozen dessert that comes in lots of flavours.

REBEL GiRLS OF ITALY

Artist **Artemisia Gentileschi** (b. 1593) painted historical scenes with brilliant colours. She's famed for portraying powerful women in her works, at a time when this was rare.

High on a hill above Florence, **Margherita Hack** (b. 1922) scanned the skies through a huge telescope, studying the stars. She became Italy's first woman director of an astronomical observatory.

Sofia

I love horse riding and judo

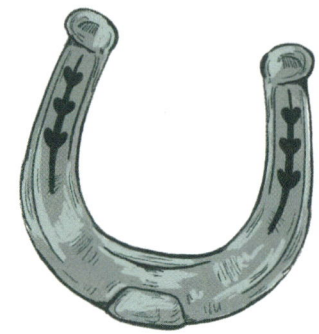

Age: 8

My home:
I live with my mom, my dad, and my brother, Davide (3). I have my own room. It has photos of me when I was little in Canada on the walls. We moved back here when I was six. My drawings are everywhere, too. They are mostly of horses and other animals. My favourite thing in my room is the bunk bed that my parents made for me out of wood in Canada and shipped back here!

My city:
Trento is a beautiful old city in the Alps. We have a medieval castle and are surrounded by mountains. There are lots of places where you can have good pizza and ice cream. During the winter you can ski, and during the summer you can go to the lakes. Lake Garda is less than an hour away by car.

I live in the Tyrol region of Italy, where both Italian and German are widely spoken. At my school some subjects are taught completely in English (like maths, music, science, and English), and some others are in Italian (like history, Italian, and religious studies). From this year we'll spend a few hours of school speaking in German, too.

The mountains can be cold, but when it's warm enough, I travel to school by bike. Otherwise I go by car or on the back of my parents' motorbike. When it snows I love to ski.

I do judo twice a week. I tried lots of other sports before my mom asked if I wanted to give judo a try. She used to do it when she was younger and thought I might like it. I like wearing the *judogi*, meeting new friends, practising with them, and learning how to defend myself.

I absolutely love horses, and I have weekly riding lessons during the warmer months. I would like to work in a riding school and become a horse-riding champion when I'm older!

I make sure I find time to draw and read every day. I like reading comics and books about animals, and I draw during break time at school. My friends and I draw together when we have playdates, too. We listen to music, play board games, and we play outside.

Carnival is a giant, magical party. It happens here every year, just before Lent. The streets fill with people in fabulous, elaborate costumes, celebrating with music, and joining parades in big, decorated wagons. The costumes are meant to scare away the harsh winter to make way for a prosperous spring.

REBEL GIRL SUPERPOWER
MAKING INSTANT CONNECTIONS WITH ANIMALS

"I was nervous at first, but once I tried judo, I loved it!"

The Netherlands

This small but densely populated country borders Germany and Belgium in Northern Europe. Its name means "lower countries". It is so low lying that it is in constant danger from being battered by the North Sea. A clever system of defence, using dams, dykes, levees, and locks, keeps it above the waterline. It is a very flat place, with a landscape covered in canals, lakes, and rivers. This flat terrain is ideal for cycling, which is a huge part of the culture – there are more bikes than there are people in the Netherlands!

Tulip Central
Around 90 per cent of the world's tulips are produced here, with billions of bulbs sold overseas every year. The 1630s saw Tulip Mania, when the price of tulips climbed higher and higher. It is said that during this time, the Semper Augustus tulip, a now-extinct variety that had red and white petals, cost as much a house!

Did you know?
Windmills were once used to power pumps that drained water from the land. There are still more than 1,000 windmills, many still in use.

King's Day
To celebrate the birthday of the King of the Netherlands, every year Dutch people celebrate Koningsdag, or King's Day (or Koninginnedag, Queen's Day, if the monarch is a woman). The streets are filled with parties, music, and dancing. Orange is symbolic of the Dutch Royal Family, and so partygoers will wear the colour – or they might even dye their hair orange for the occasion!

Sea Level
About a third of the country is below sea level, meaning that it is lower than the average height of the sea. This puts the Netherlands at risk of serious flooding. But there are around 3,600 kilometres of long walls called dykes that protect the land. There are also dams, levees, and pumping stations – some powered by windmills! – that help to control water and avoid flooding.

FAST FACTS

Official Name: Kingdom of the Netherlands

Capital: Amsterdam

Location: Northwestern Europe

Border Countries: Belgium, Germany

Official Language: Dutch

Currency: Euro

Population: 18 million

Area: 41,543 km^2

Wheely Good Cheese!

Cheese is a big deal here. Two of the most famous cheeses, Edam and Gouda, are named after the towns in which they're made. In the warmer months of the year, you can visit a cheese market, where dairy farmers haul huge wheels of cheese to be sold. At Alkmaar Market, the cheese wheels are lugged around in barrows, weighed, and then taken away in horse-drawn wagons.

AMSTERDAM

Paintings and Pottery

Visiting the Rijksmuseum, the national museum of the Netherlands, in Amsterdam, you can discover some true masterpieces. Works by artists such as Rembrandt, Johannes Vermeer, and Judith Leyster are proudly displayed. These creators were part of the Dutch Golden Age. The collection also includes delftware, a type of pottery from the Dutch city of Delft, known for its blue and white patterns.

Cycling Culture

Cycling has freewheeled its way deep into Dutch culture, helping people to travel and stay healthy while caring for the environment. The Dutch government has pledged to reduce greenhouse gas emissions by around 60 per cent by 2030. It prioritises cycling to help achieve this goal. Most Dutch towns and cities have cycling routes in dedicated lanes, and plenty of bike parking to encourage people to jump on their bike instead of driving!

REBEL GIRLS OF THE NETHERLANDS

Passionate about fighting climate change **Bernice Notenboom** (b. 1962) made history as the first woman on skis to reach both the North and South Poles as well as the Siberian Pole of Cold.

Sifan Hassan (b. 1993) is a middle- and long-distance runner. She completed a unique triple at the Tokyo 2020 Olympic Games, winning gold medals in both the 5,000 metres and 10,000 metres, and a bronze medal for the 1,500 metres.

Liv

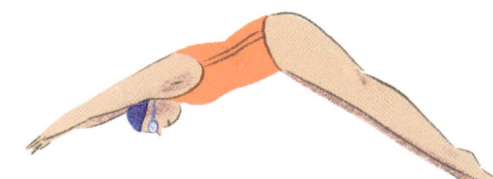

I'm happiest when I'm free to do my thing

"I love being around my favourite people more than anything."

My greatest passion is singing and playing guitar. I have guitar lessons once a week. I love listening to music and writing my own songs, and I play in a band with my older brother, too.

We are a chaotic, music-loving family. Even our two cats are named after musicians: Billie (for Billie Holiday) and Jimi (for Jimi Hendrix). Billie is round and black and white, and Jimi is a little tiger.

I have recently been diagnosed with Lyme disease. It went undetected for a long time and has been making me feel very weak and tired, so I ride on the back of my mum's bike to school.

My friends and I talk to each other about everything, and we really love to laugh. We play outside together, climb trees, and enjoy going swimming and practising our diving. We also love painting and dancing.

I have a tiny bedroom, filled with my own paintings, photos, posters, and, of course – my guitars. I love spending time on my bed in the evening writing, sketching, or reading. I love books with tension.

I want to be a singer-songwriter and a guitar player. I'm inspired by Billie Eilish and Alice Phoebe Lou: two strong, individual musicians who have their very own style. I'm proud that I am getting better at recording songs myself on my recording programme. It's nice to make progress.

Age: 11

My family:
I live with my mum, dad, my sister, Juna (13), my 17-year-old brother, Lou, and our two cats. We speak German and Dutch at home, and Dutch at school.

My city:
Maastricht is a beautiful, old city in the south of the Netherlands, bisected by the River Meuse. My city is full of beautiful historical buildings and houses, pretty squares, and restaurants.

Maeve

I like to read about trailblazers

"If I had a pet I would either want a dog, a hamster, or an axolotl."

Age: 8

My home:
I live with my mom, my dad, and my brother, Jude (10). My favourite thing in my bedroom is my bulletin board, because I put up pictures of me and my friends on it. I have a Taylor Swift poster on my wall and different LEGO® sets and toys up on shelves.

My town:
Amstelveen is a town right next to Amsterdam. There are around 97,000 people that live here, but almost one-third of the people are from other countries. My family moved here from the United States before I was born. It has a lot of canals, it rains a lot, and there are a few old windmills around. Most people live in semi-detached or terraced houses and some people live in apartment buildings.

There are a lot of bike paths here, and most people get around on bikes, *bakfiets* (cargo bikes with big boxes on the front of them that kids can ride in), or by tram.

There are 15 kids in my class. They are from all over the world because I go to an international school. We speak English at school but I also go to Dutch lessons. We have recess outside in the playground twice a day, and I eat lunch in a cafeteria.

We celebrate Koningsdag (King's Day) here. It is a celebration of our King's birthday. Everybody wears orange, the colour of the Royal Family, and most people have the day off from school or work. It's traditional to set up a little stall and sell things. Kids usually sell old toys or homemade food, or they can run games or do performances to try to earn money.

This year I joined the choir and the percussion group as extra activities at school. I am proud of how much my violin playing has improved in the year I have been learning.

I love art and I'm in the art club at school. I like being creative with free drawing, and I enjoy building things like little dioramas, or working with clay. I recently did a really beautiful painting like Van Gogh's *Starry Night over the Rhône* that I am very proud of.

I would love to be a teacher when I'm older. I would get to design and plan fun and interesting projects for my class to work on. It would be cool to teach my students all the classic subjects as well as technology skills, like using a green screen and making movies.

REBEL GIRL SUPERPOWER

DETERMINATION – GIVING THINGS MY ALL

Let's Go to Lisbon

Lisbon is a pastel-coloured city that has been inhabited for around 3,000 years. Its location on the mouth of the Tagus River has made it an important place for trade throughout history. Overtourism has become an issue in the last few years, so learning to speak a bit of Portuguese and supporting small businesses is extra helpful when traveling in Lisbon.

Portugal

The Republic of Portugal is attached to Spain by one of the longest uninterrupted borders in Europe. Cabo da Roca, a cliff that looks out over the Atlantic Ocean, is the most western point of the continent of Europe. To the north are the Estrela mountains, where people can hike in summer and ski in winter. To the south is the Algarve, a beach destination that is a hotspot for tourists. At 17.2 kilometres, the Vasco da Gama bridge is the longest bridge in in the EU. Thousands of runners have to tackle its length each year during the Lisbon Marathon!

Amazing *Azulejo*

The Portuguese art of painting tiles with intricate patterns is known as *azulejo*, which means "little stone". It is influenced by Islamic cultures, and its origins began in the 16th century in Lisbon. The beautiful art can be found across different churches, schools, and palaces.

FAST FACTS

Capital: Lisbon

Location: Europe

Border Countries: Spain

Official Language: Portuguese

Currency: Euro

Population: 10.7 million

Area: 92,090 km²

Did you know?
The oldest bookshop in the world is in Lisbon. Livraria Bertrand was founded in 1732 by two French brothers.

132

Portuguese Islands

In the Atlantic Ocean, off the coast of Africa and Europe, lies the island chain of the Azores. Created by volcanoes, it is dotted with stunning waterfalls, hot springs, and the highest mountain in Portugal, Mount Pico. The island chain of Madeira lies to the west of the Azores. Here you'll find more natural wonders, including a rainforest that is around 20 million years old: the Laurisilva Forest.

AZORES

Tasty Treats

A true Portuguese delicacy is a sweet tart called a *Pastel de Nata*. It's a crispy cup of pastry that's filled with a creamy egg custard. While different eateries now bake their own version of the tasty treat, the original recipe was passed from a group of monks to a family business in the 19th century. It has been kept a closely guarded secret ever since.

Language

For more than five centuries, Portugal colonized many countries around the world, which is why Portuguese is still the official language in places like Brazil, Angola, and Mozambique. There are around 220 million people in the world today who speak Portuguese, with the vast majority of those people living in Brazil. There are also large communities in the United States that speak Portuguese.

REBEL GIRLS OF PORTUGAL

Born in Lisbon, artist **Paula Rego** (b. 1935) specialized in creating portraits of people inspired by fairy tales. Her exciting work helped to change the face of the art world forever.

Carmen Miranda (b. 1909) was a Portuguese-born singer and actress. She became one of the biggest names in Brazil thanks to her performances in radio, casinos and in international cinema and musicals.

Cool Waves!

There is a huge variety of waves off the coast of Portugal, so it is a fantastic place to surf. The west coast town of Nazaré is home to record-breaking waves, some of the biggest in the world. It is dangerous, but perfect for daredevil surfers looking for a challenge. The coast across the south of the country brings gentler waves, making it good for beginners.

CASCAIS PORTUGAL

Age: 10

My home:
I live with my mum, my dad, my three brothers, Nicolas (18), Stéphane (16), and Alexandre (13), and our puppy, Zuma. My bedroom is painted pink, with white furniture and lots of picture frames with photos of family and friends. It has the best view in the house. I love to watch the sunset from my window.

My town:
Cascais is a coastal resort town just west of Lisbon. It is very small. I love the fact that it is right by the sea. The sea always makes me feel happy, and so do the beautiful sunsets. Cascais is famous for Santini ice cream which I love, and sardines which I really dislike.

Nathalie

My friends call me Nat

¶ I love to run across the fields of yellow flowers near my house. I take my beautiful dog, Zuma. It's the best feeling. It makes me feel really free, and the air is clean and fresh. I always help to take care of Zuma. I would love to be a vet when I'm older.

¶ Where I live is very pretty. There are so many different trees, plants, fruits, and loads of flowers. There are various species of birds, lots of rabbits, ducks, butterflies, and the odd cat wandering around. A blue macaw comes at times, and once there was even a snake!

¶ I part-own a horse called Guapa. She is a 13-year-old mare with a brown, shiny coat, and a black wavy mane and tail. She is a mix of Lusitano (a Portuguese breed), and thoroughbred. She is a bit of a diva, who needs plenty of exercise and only likes one other horse. I love jumping with Guapa; 80 centimetres is my record!

¶ We always pick a theme for my birthday. Last year it was dogs, this year it will be horses. My mum decorates the breakfast table to match, and sometimes I even get specially shaped cookies. Since it's a special day, I get to choose whatever I want to for breakfast, lunch, and dinner.

¶ I play football in my school team. I am an Arsenal fan like my older brother. When I'm allowed to, I watch the matches on TV with him, dressed in my Arsenal shirt.

¶ I'm in the Community Service club at school. We raise money for those not as fortunate as us by holding bake sales, selling chocolates, and setting up a "Christmas Wish Tree" – you take an ornament off the tree and buy the toy written on the ornament for a child in an orphanage.

REBEL GIRL SUPERPOWER: MY KINDNESS

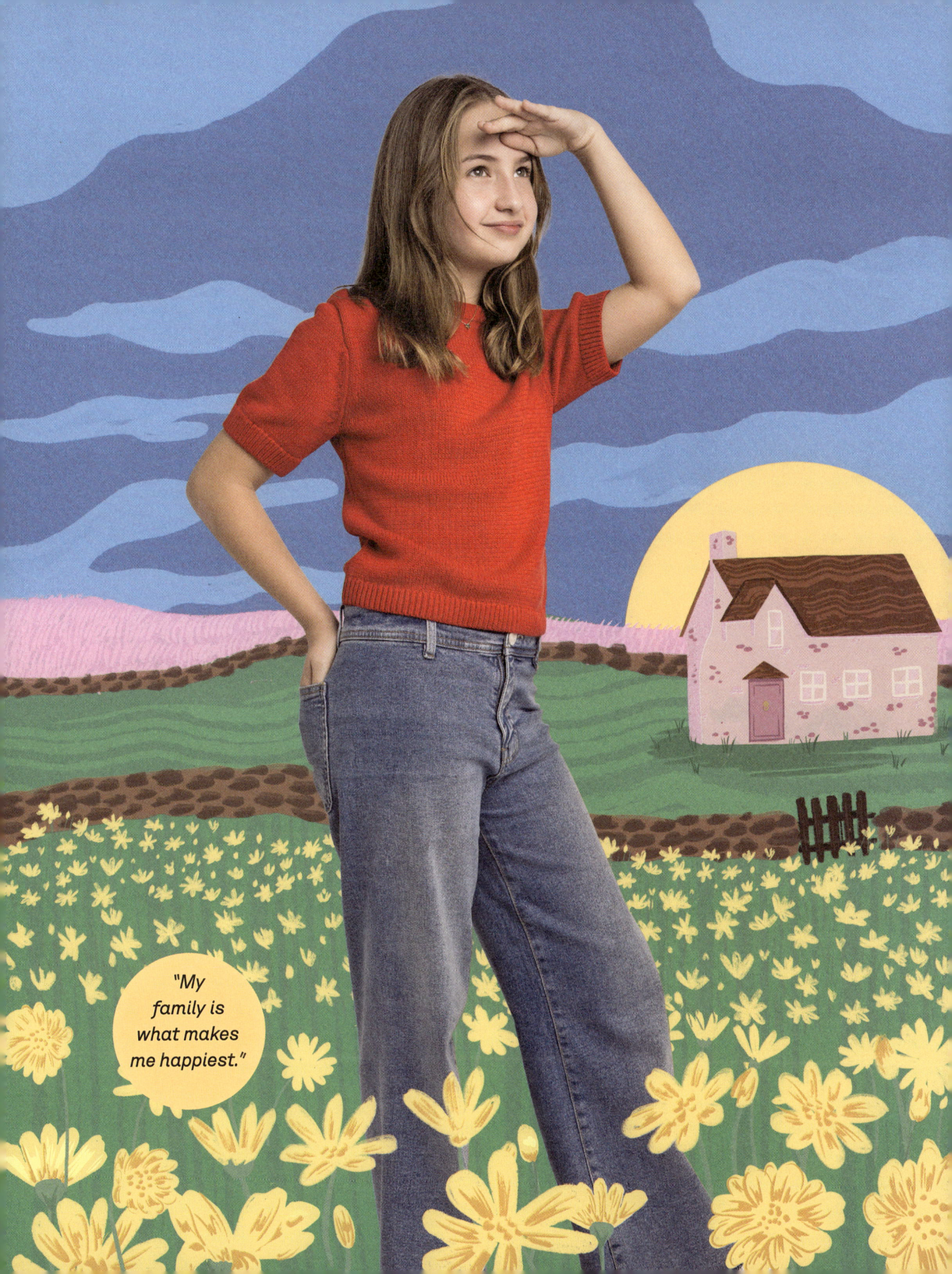

Slovakia

Did you know?
Bratislava is only 60 kilometres from Vienna, Austria's capital. That is the shortest distance between capital cities in the world.

Slovakia is a landlocked country in Central Europe, where the peaks and troughs of the Carpathian Mountains dominate the top portion of the landmass. Slovakia and Czechia were part of the same country – Czechoslovakia – from 1918 until 1992, when they peacefully dissolved into two independent states. Although it is quite young as a nation, Slovakia has a rich cultural history and people are proud of their folkloric traditions. Most people speak Slovak, but a Hungarian-speaking community makes up nearly 10 per cent of the population.

Towers and Turrets

There are around 180 castles in Slovakia. Some are ruins, such as Devín Castle, built in 864 CE. Others, like the pretty, turreted Bojnice Castle, are very well preserved. In the capital, Bratislava, the skyline is changing thanks to a different kind of tower – the skyscraper. Sky Park, designed by renowned architect Dame Zaha Hadid, is just one of the city's futuristic new projects.

Fairy-tale Forests

Around 40 per cent of Slovakia is carpeted by forests of beech, pine, and spruce trees. It is a perfect place for wildlife to thrive, including some big beasts like Eurasian lynx and bears. The forest floor is a fantastic place to spot mushrooms. Foraging for edible varieties, such as chanterelles, is a national pastime – but should never be tried by anyone who doesn't know how to spot the poisonous kinds too.

FAST FACTS

Official Name: Slovak Republic

Capital: Bratislava

Border Countries: Austria, Czechia, Hungary, Poland, Ukraine

Location: Central Europe

Official Language: Slovak

Currency: Euro

Population: 5.4 million

Area: 49,035 km²

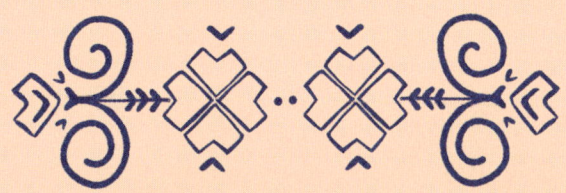

Maypole Mayhem
To mark the beginning of the month of May, when the warmer months of the year begin, a tradition in Slovakia is to put up a maypole. This is a tall birch, fir, or spruce tree, cleaned of branches and leaves, that is mounted in the centre of a town or village. Wreaths and ribbons are attached to the top of the maypole, and it is customary for people to sing and dance around it.

TATRA MOUNTAINS

Natural Beauty
From the rugged snowy peaks of the Tatra Mountains on the border with Poland to underground caves with incredible stalactites and stalagmites like Domica Cave, Slovakia is filled with natural havens. There are more than 1,600 mineral springs, which are said to have healing properties. The Liptov and Tatras regions are great places to experience the waterparks and spas that make use of the natural water sources found in Slovakia.

Pioneers on Ice
Slovakia is a nation of ice hockey fans, and in 2025, Dolný Kubín was chosen as the host city for the first ever Para Ice Hockey Women's World Championships. Six teams of athletes came together to compete in the historic event, including Team World, which was made up of players from nine different nations across Asia and Europe, and included two Slovakian players. Slovakian defender Ema Simakova was only 16 years old when she took to the ice in front of an enthusiastic home crowd!

DOMICA CAVES

REBEL GIRLS OF SLOVAKIA

Maria Bellova (b. 1885) was the first ever woman to become a doctor in Slovakia, in 1910. She devoted her life to treating children suffering from a deadly disease called tuberculosis.

Sometimes referred to as "the first feminist of Slovakia", **Elena Maróthy-Šoltésová** (b. 1855) was a writer who campaigned for the rights of women in her country.

Anna

I read and draw whenever I can

BRATISLAVA SLOVAKIA

Age: 8

My home:
I live with my mom, dad, and two sisters, Mila (7), and Nina (4). My sisters and I share a bedroom and a playroom, which we have decorated with all our colourful craft projects and books. It gets really messy!

My city:
Bratislava is the capital city of Slovakia. It lies on the Danube River, and is the only national capital in the world to border two foreign countries: Austria and Hungary. We have a beautiful pedestrianized old town and an amazing castle on a hill overlooking the city.

When I'm at home I speak Slovak, my native language, with my mom, and English with my dad and sisters. We speak both English and Slovak at school. I attend an international school. It is so fun to learn alongside kids from so many different backgrounds.

I read absolutely everywhere: at the breakfast table, in the car, on the toilet, in bed – even when I'm walking along the street! I like comics, encyclopedias, and diaries best. I'm inspired by Anne Frank. I loved reading her diary and learning about her important story.

My favourite meal is *bryndzové halušky*, which is a traditional dish made with potato dumplings and sheep's cheese. It's really creamy and rich, and it can be served with small pieces of crispy bacon on top. It's delicious!

I love to draw manga figures. I draw teenagers in manga style, practising the details like hands and eyes over and over. It takes a lot of repetition to get better. I love the detail that you can find in manga comics, and the fact that you can create new characters and whole worlds with a pen and paper. It can be hard if I don't have the right inspiration or mindset, but I keep trying.

I am learning the piano in my spare time, and I am in the art, dance, and coding clubs at school. Sports wise, I enjoy climbing, playing golf, and watching ice hockey with my dad.

REBEL GIRL SUPERPOWER: BEING A GOOD FRIEND

"I don't know what I want to be yet, but what I do know is that I would like to help other people and our planet."

Spain

Bordered by Portugal to the west, and France to the north, Spain sits in the southwest of Europe. The Canary Islands in the Atlantic Ocean, and the Balearic Islands in the Mediterranean Sea, also form part of this sunny country. From the peaks and valleys of the Pyrenees mountains in the north to the scorching southern deserts, Spain has amazing sights to see. The country is peppered with busy cities, such as Barcelona on the northeast coast, Bilbao to the north, and Madrid, the capital, that sits in the middle.

A Spanish Breed

The Andalusian horse, known in Spain as *"Pura Raza Española"*, which means "Spanish pure breed", is a type of horse that originated in Spain and is now revered all over the world. A clever animal with a gentle temperament and a strong frame, it's widely thought of as one of best types of horse to ride, and has been the pride of Spain for centuries.

A Taste of Spain

Tapas, small plates of food, such as olives, padron peppers, and fried potatoes, are served before a main meal. Each area of Spain has its own special types, so there are hundreds of different options to choose from. Paella is another traditional dish, made with rice, that has different ingredients depending on the region.

Fabulous Flamenco

Flamenco dancing derives from the culture of Andalusian Roma people in southern Spain. It is accompanied by flamenco music, led by guitar and people clapping. A vocalist will sing, while the dancer moves their body, to help tell a story. Women dancers traditionally wear dresses that are adorned with ruffles. One of the most famous dancers was Carmen Amaya, known for her powerful moves.

FAST FACTS

Capital: Madrid

Location: Southern and Western Europe

Border Countries: Andorra, France, Gibraltar, Morocco, Portugal

Official Language: Spanish

Currency: Euro

Population: 48.8 million

Area: 505,370 km^2

Something to Celebrate!

There is always a reason to celebrate in Spain! La Tomatina is a huge food fight, in which the town of Buñol is covered with almost a tonne of pulped tomato each year. At Las Fallas, huge wooden and cardboard statues are burned in bonfires that light up the night sky. Semana Santa celebrates the last week before the Christian holiday of Easter Sunday.

Did you know? Festivals are celebrated throughout the year here, many rooted in Catholicism, a religion that has long been part of Spanish culture.

The Strait of Gibraltar

The body of water between Spain and Morocco – the Strait of Gibraltar – is only 14 kilometres across. This relatively short distance means that Spain is an important stop on the way for birds, such as black kites, storks, and eagles, migrating between Europe and Africa. It's also home to magnificent mammals roaming its landscape, including wolves, lynxes, wildcats, foxes, and deer.

LA SAGRADA FAMÍLIA

Inspiring Architecture

Spain boasts some truly awe-inspiring architecture, showcasing a dramatic blend of Islamic, Christian, and Gothic influences. Barcelona is dominated by buildings designed by Antoni Gaudí, including La Sagrada Família, a Roman Catholic church so intricate and detailed it has been in construction since 1882 and is still not yet complete. Gaudí called his style "Hispano-Saracenic-Gothic" and was inspired by nature and geometry.

REBEL GIRLS OF SPAIN

Famously known as one of the greatest Flamenco dancers of all time, **Carmen Amaya** (b. 1918) was the first woman to dance steps previously only mastered by male dancers. She made her debut at just six years old!

Patricia Campos Doménech (b. 1977) is an association football coach and former aviator in the Spanish Navy. After leaving the Navy, Patricia bravely came out as a lesbian, fully aware of the stigmas faced by LGBTQ+ activists in the military.

Helena

My family calls me Hele

Age: 8

My home:
I live with my parents and my brother, Martin (9). I share a room with him, decorated with rockets and planets. Valentina Tereshkova, the first woman to go to space, is so inspiring to me! I have lots of stuffed animals. My favourite is Zorrín, a fox cub.

My town:
La Puebla de Almoradiel is a small town in central Spain. It has several bridges and squares, and a river that runs through it. The people are friendly and we all know each other. Most of my family lives here, too. We are surrounded by vineyards and it smells very nice! Nearby Toledo was also an important old city where many kings lived. I travel there a lot because it is close and I really like its history.

The fair is my favourite tradition in our town. It lasts for four days in September. It starts with a procession, and lots of people visit the hermitage of Christ (a small shrine-like chapel, up a hill). Then, we get to go on the fairground rides! I buy candyfloss, there are concerts, and we go to bed very late. There is no school and all the children join in the fun.

My favourite school days are when I have PE, I really like sports. I go out on my bike at weekends, and I'm good at skipping. I like to challenge myself and set new records. I have belonged to my local athletics club for two years. This year, I'll be old enough to enter competitions.

I really like to stay busy in my spare time. I go to storytelling sessions at the library, roller-skate at the rink near my house, or play tag or dodgeball. When it's raining, I experiment with makeup, cooking, painting, or drawing. And I love theme parks! On Fridays we go to the playground for older children and they play music to dance to. My brother and my cousin come, too. It's the best day.

I look forward to family time, having board game and computer game tournaments, or simply enjoying big meals with my cousins and grandparents. Our grandparents live nearby and I see them a lot. They have a beautiful dog named Luca; she looks like a fox. Sometimes I take her for a walk or help my grandfather to bathe her. I like helping my grandmother in the kitchen. Her Spanish omelette is the best!

I love reading stories from Greek mythology. The myth about the Trojan Horse is my favourite; I especially like Helen of Troy, because we share a name. I enjoy any books about animals and mythological beings. Lately I've been reading the *Unicornia* and *Monster School* books.

REBEL GIRL SUPERPOWER: MY ENERGY! I DO WHAT I WANT, AND I SING LOUDLY

"Magic means having the power to do special things, like fly, or turn into an animal."

Alba

I give everything my all

I love both of my bedrooms. My room at Dad's is so cosy; the decor suits someone my age, but it still has touches of my room from when I was little. My bed at Mum's has a sofa on the bottom. It is made up with sheets from Paris. I have always dreamed of visiting one day. It looks so pretty. I'd love to see its sites and eat macarons at a pavement café!

I go to the same German school my mum went to. We learn in German and follow German traditions, though we also speak Spanish and Catalan. We celebrate a Culture Day every year. Each child brings a typical dish from their culture. I like learning about other countries.

We make living between two homes work. On weekdays, I meet my dad at a café at 7:30am. We drop my little sister off at daycare, then Dad drives me to school. My mum comes to take me to my after-school clubs. I train 12.5 hours a week at my artistic gymnastics club, and I also do an hour of dance. I'm usually home by 9pm.

The best thing about gymnastics is my friends. We have so much fun. We go trampolining, have sleepovers, skate, and just hang out. Despite our busy schedules, we always find time to be together. I love talking to them, whether it's about important topics like history and social injustices, or simply TV shows we want to watch.

I look forward to Diada de Sant Jordi every year, it's our local festival honouring Catalonia's patron saint, Saint George. On this day, it's customary to give a rose or a book to someone special in our lives. The streets fill with stalls selling books and flowers, and balconies all over the city are decorated with beautiful paper roses. As a book lover, it's my favourite celebration!

Age: 12

My home:
I split my time between my parents' houses. It's just me at my mum's. I have a little sister, Clàudia (3), at my dad's. I love playing with her and I love her very much. I'm lucky enough to have my own room at both houses!

My city:
To me, Barcelona is a beautiful city with the perfect climate! It is the capital of Catalonia, which is a self-governing region of northeastern Spain with an important history. We have our own language (Catalan), and a strong cultural identity. Forming human towers called "castells" is an amazing Catalan tradition originating in the 18th Century.

"There are many things that scare me in gymnastics, but I try to be brave and do them."

Martina

I always try to be honest

SPAIN — PONFERRADA

Age: 11

My home:
I live with my parents and have my own room, which is painted pink! I have a trundle bed so we can wheel out the second mattress underneath mine when I have friends to sleep over. I have a super cool lamp and a shelf where I display my favourite things.

My city:
Ponferrada is a small, historic city surrounded by mountains, in northwestern Spain. It has a very cool ancient Templar castle, an ancient Roman goldmine, called Las Médulas, and a river that cuts through the upper and lower areas of the city. I live in the lower area, where my school is. We have very cold winters and very hot summers.

My city is on the Camino de Santiago, an ancient Catholic pilgrimage route. People from all over the world still walk the 790 kilometres from the Pyrenees mountains in France to the town in Spain where they believe the bones of Saint James are buried.

We go to the nearby city of León every Easter, to watch the Holy Week processions. Large, handmade *pasos* (floats) depict scenes from Jesus's last days. Some of the floats are centuries old. My favourite scene is the one with Saint Veronica. At home, my family gathers outside in the garden to pray and reflect on how to be the best versions of ourselves.

I'm taking tennis lessons after school. I'm happiest when I'm on the court, in the fresh air! I love going to watch sports matches with my parents, especially football. Being with family and friends is the best feeling. My friends and I love going to the shopping centre in town. We go to the cinema, or just to get food. In summer, we meet up to go to the swimming pool.

I'm passionate about learning English, and reading new books. My favourites are *A Door with Three Locks* by Sonia Fernández-Vidal, and *Murder Most Unladylike* by Robin Stevens. I like reading mysteries because I want to be a criminologist, a forensic scientist, or a psychologist when I grow up.

I have a pet bird called Rodri. I keep him at my grandparents' house. I see him every weekend. He is brown and very vocal. He absolutely loves to sing. If he doesn't sing for a day my grandparents start worrying!

> "I'm proud that I'm good at maths and English."

Sweden

In the Swedish summer, days are long and the sun shines for hours over thousands of sparkling lakes. In winter, thick snow is common – perfect for building giant snowmen! The Kingdom of Sweden – as it is officially named – is both one of the largest and the least populated countries in Europe. It is among the world leaders in recycling, and has a reputation for prioritizing outdoor play and hobbies in all weather. No wonder it is often known as being one of the happiest countries in the world to live in.

Traditional carved wooden Dala horses are a familiar sight in Sweden! Painted in bright colours and patterns, they are a national symbol of craftsmanship.

Nature and Wildlife
Sweden has vast forests covering more than 60 per cent of its land. Around 100,000 lakes and amazing mountain scenery make it a popular place for outdoor sports, such as skiing, canoeing, and ice-skating. Sweden is home to many wild animals, including bears, moose, reindeer, and even wolves!

Arctic Skies
The sun doesn't set in the northern part of Sweden in summer! This is called the "Midnight Sun". In winter, it is completely dark for several weeks, especially in the far north. This is called the "Polar Night". The spectacular natural light shows visible in northern Sweden are known as the "Aurora Borealis", or the "Northern Lights".

FAST FACTS

Capital: Stockholm

Location: Scandinavia, Northern Europe

Border Countries: Finland, Norway

Official Language: Swedish

Currency: Swedish Krona

Population: 10.57 million

Area: 450,295 km²

Did you know?
Swedish inventor Alfred Nobel created *The Nobel Prize* to recognize people whose work offers the greatest benefit to humankind.

Feeling Peckish?
You might have tried *köttbullar* (Swedish meatballs), which are often served with potatoes and lingonberry jam, but have you heard of *surströmming*? It is a very strong-smelling type of fermented fish enjoyed in northern Sweden. It was invented during the salt shortage of the 16th century and is said to be as stinky as it is yummy!

Scandi Style
Crafting skills are revered in Sweden, and the country is known for minimalist designs that emphasize use of natural materials like wood and glass. Swedish design is also famous for its simplicity, and IKEA, the homeware store that sells flat-pack furniture, has exported simple Swedish design around the world at affordable prices.

City of Islands
Stockholm is a unique capital city built on 14 islands connected by 57 bridges. All that water has earned it the nickname, "Venice of the North". But some of its finest treasures lie underground: the tunnels and stations of the 110-kilometre metro network are full of art and sculptures.

Education
In Sweden, children typically start school at age six or seven. All Swedish school pupils between the ages of 6–16 receive a free, nutritious school lunch every day.

STOCKHOLM

Fika Time!
Fika (pronounced "fee-ka") is a special Swedish tradition. It's a time to take a break and enjoy coffee or tea with a sweet treat like cinnamon buns. *Fika* is not just about food; it's about taking time to relax and chat with friends.

REBEL GIRLS OF SWEDEN

Sara Sjöström (b. 1993), was 14 when she won her first international gold medal for swimming. She is now one of the most decorated sprint swimmers of all time.

Author **Astrid Lindgren** (b. 1907) is best known for creating Pippi Longstocking, a strong, independent, and adventurous girl, who challenges gender norms and lives life on her own terms.

Clara

It's important to be a good friend

LULEÅ
SWEDEN

I love being in nature and am in an orienteering club. In summer, we take our paddleboard over the water from our house to the little beach where the river meets the sea. In winter, I often go ice skating on the same river when it freezes over! We also go alpine and cross-country skiing.

I speak Swedish at home and at school. My grandparents also speak Meänkieli: a mixture of Swedish and Finnish spoken in the Tornedalian region in northern Sweden. "*Lagom*" is a typical Swedish word. It means "not too much and not too little, but just right" – like when you get exactly the perfect amount of ice cream!

We celebrate Midsummer in June on the longest day of the year, when it is light almost all day and night here. Families and friends all get together for a picnic. We wear flower crowns on our heads and dance around a big maypole. The dancing is really fun – we get to hop about like frogs in one traditional dance!

I'm a *trivselledare* at school. A *trivselledare* is a school kid whose responsibility it is to organize and run games at break so that everyone can play together. This stops anyone from feeling left out and prevents bullying.

I play on a basketball team in my spare time. My mom is the coach! My town has the best women's basketball team in Sweden and I enjoy watching live matches when I can. I also play football and enjoy climbing.

Age: 9

My home:
I live with my mom, my dad, and my younger sister, Thea (7). I have my own bedroom in the basement. It's painted purple! I chose the paint colour myself and I love being on my own floor.

My town:
Luleå is a small town in northern Sweden, surrounded by forests and lakes. In winter, there is lots of snow and you can sometimes see reindeer and the Northern Lights, which Sweden is famous for.

"A friend in my class fled to Sweden because of the war in Ukraine. Sometimes I wonder how girls in war zones are living their lives."

Switzerland

A small, landlocked country in the heart of Europe, Switzerland is one of the richest countries in the world. It is famous for its banks, its exports, such as chocolate and watches, and its peaceful way of life. The country has more than 1,500 clean lakes nestled among mountains, including Lake Geneva, which is the largest in Western Europe. Switzerland is home to 9 million people who overwhelmingly love nature – 90 per cent of Swiss people believe that protected wilderness is important!

Four Official Languages

Switzerland is a multilingual country, with four official languages. German is spoken by the majority of people, while French, Italian, and Romansh are spoken in specific regions. People in the western part of Switzerland speak French, while in the southern region, people speak Italian.

Prioritizing Peace

Switzerland has been neutral in wars for more than 200 years, meaning it doesn't take sides in conflicts. Ninety-one per cent of Swiss citizens support neutrality, though the policy is also accused of condoning unethical regimes. Also based in the country is the International Red Cross, an organization dedicated to helping all people affected by war.

Mighty Mountains

The Swiss Alps and Jura Mountains cover more than 60 per cent of Switzerland. With a bit of luck you might spot ibex, chamois, marmots, lynx, and wolves on their slopes. The beautiful, pyramid-shaped Matterhorn is the world's most photographed mountain. It even inspired the shape of a famous Swiss chocolate bar: Toblerone!

FAST FACTS

Official Name: Swiss Confederation

Seat of Government: Bern

Border Countries: Austria, France, Germany, Italy, Liechtenstein

Official Languages: German, French, Italian, Romansh

Currency: Swiss Franc

Population: 9 million

Area: 41,277 km²

Did you know? Switzerland and the Vatican City are the only two countries to have square flags.

LAKE GENEVA

Chocolate and Cheese
Switzerland's cows graze in unpolluted alpine pastures. Perhaps it is their milk that makes Swiss cheese and chocolate so delicious! Swiss people have been making chocolate since the 19th century. Today, the country produces about 180,000 tonnes of it each year. Around 180 types of cheese are produced here, including Gruyère, used in fondue, and Emmental, known for its holes.

Tick Tock!
Switzerland is famous for producing some of the finest watches in the world. The Swiss watchmaking industry dates back to the 16th century, and today Switzerland is home to more than 500 watch companies, contributing around £16 billion to the Swiss economy.

The Great Outdoors
Switzerland's ski resorts attract about 1.5 million people every year. During the summer, the country's 65,000 kilometres of hiking trails and 9,000 kilometres of biking routes offer endless adventures in nature. Switzerland is also famous for its scenic train rides, like the Glacier Express®, which offers breathtaking views of the mountains and valleys.

REBEL GIRLS OF SWITZERLAND

Paralympic athlete **Abassia Rahmani** (b. 1992) is the first Swiss female blade runner. She had both legs amputated at the age of 16, but didn't let that stop her love of sport. She now competes internationally on blades.

Marthe Gosteli (b. 1917) led the fight for Swiss women's right to vote, then went on to create an archive of women's biographies and history. She was awarded the Swiss Human Rights Award in 2011.

Alice

I love to perform

Age: 11

My home:
I live with my mum, my dad, and my little sister (9). We moved house recently and now I have my own room, with space to sing and dance. I have posters of singers I like on the wall.

My city:
Lausanne is a beautiful city on a big lake. It is the official Olympic Capital, where the Olympic headquarters and museum are based. I love visiting the antique medals, equipment, and sports kits. I'm mainly interested in gymnastics, basketball, athletics, and skiing.

We speak French at school, and we're learning German and English. English class is easy for me; my mum is from England so I can practise at home! My dad is from the French-speaking part of Switzerland. I speak to my little sister in either language depending on my mood.

I'm in an athletics club and I really like longer runs as well as sprints. Sometimes I win medals at my running competitions and it makes me feel really proud of myself.

Our family eats local food where possible. Luckily that includes cheese fondue – yum! A little bit of alcohol is used to prepare it, but it's still OK for children. Fondue is made differently in different regions of France and Switzerland, but where I live it's "*moitié-moitié*", which means "half and half". It's half Gruyère cheese and half Vacherin cheese.

I'm passionate about singing and acting. I have a microphone and DJ set and I dance and sing along, pretending I'm Taylor Swift. I went to see her in concert and still have the friendship bracelets on my wall. It's inspiring that she started her career when she was a young teenager. I'd love to meet her, Millie Bobby Brown, and Zendaya!

I take circus classes. The aerial acts like flat and round trapeze are my favourite. In the winter I ski a lot in the mountains near where I live – sometimes I go with friends, and sometimes it's just with my family.

Türkiye

Türkiye (formerly "Turkey") stretches across Europe and Asia, and its largest city, Istanbul, sits on a body of water called the Bosphorus Strait, which straddles the two continents. To the north lies the Black Sea, with the Aegean Sea to the west, and the Mediterranean Sea to the south. This is a place with a powerful political history, which played an important role in the Roman, Byzantine, and Ottoman empires. A sunny climate, tasty food, and lots of historical sites mean it's the world's fifth most-visited country.

Hoop Dreams

Basketball has slam-dunked its way into Turkish life, and is now one of the country's most popular sports. Men have played since the 1900s, and in 1980, the Turkish Women's Basketball League (TWBL) was set up, which now attracts top players from around the world.

Like Another World

Cappadocia in central Türkiye is a breathtaking and dramatic landscape. Ancient people realized that the volcanic rock here could be carved to create a network of underground caves and towns to live in. Above ground, there are towering rocks, shaped like enormous, skinny mushrooms. They are so whimsical that they've got a nickname: fairy chimneys! Today, visitors can take a hot-air balloon ride to make the most of the stunning views.

Did you know?

In 2022, Türkiye officially changed its name in English from "Turkey" to "Türkiye", to align closer with its name in Turkish.

FAST FACTS

Official Name: Republic of Türkiye

Capital: Ankara

Location: Europe to the west, Asia to the east

Border Countries: Armenia, Azerbaijan, Bulgaria, Georgia, Greece, Iran, Iraq, Syria

Official Language: Turkish

Currency: Turkish Lira

Population: 85.5 million

Area: 783,562 km²

Whirling Dervishes

A centuries-old dance of worship performed by a strand of Muslims called the Sufi originated here. The dancers are called whirling dervishes. They wear white and a hat made of felt. A group of them twirl on the spot in unison, their ceremonial garments flowing outwards as they move. It is a form of meditation and prayer that is only ever practised in front of an audience.

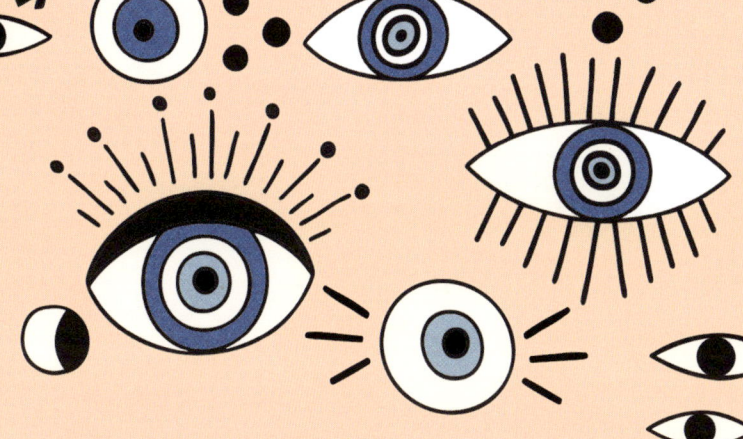

Craft and Culture

A beautiful history of arts and crafts exists in Türkiye. *Iznik*, named after the town in which it was made, is beautifully decorated pottery. Expertly woven rugs, patterned with flowers and geometric shapes and lines, are also a speciality. In particular, Türkiye is known for a blue decorative stone called the *nazar boncuğu* ("evil eye bead"). Made from molten glass, iron, and copper, it is said to ward off evil spirits and bad energy.

Delights of Türkiye

Turkish delight, a squidgy sweet treat made of starch and sugar, originated here. Its most traditional version is made with rosewater, orange, and lemon. Another sweet treat is *baklava*, a dessert made of layers of filo pastry, chopped nuts, and sweet syrup. Both are washed down nicely with some Turkish tea, served in a tulip-shaped glass.

The Biggest City

The capital city of Istanbul has a unique blend of European and Asian influences. Its fantastic sights include the Hagia Sophia, a beautiful mosque that has also been a church and a museum. The Grand Bazaar is one of the oldest and largest indoor markets in the world, with more than 4,000 shops inside it.

REBEL GIRLS OF TÜRKIYE

Dilhan Eryurt (b. 1926) became the first Turkish woman scientist to work at NASA. She went on to discover that the Sun used to be hotter than it is today, furthering our understanding of the Solar System.

Selda Bağcan (b. 1948) is a folk singer-songwriter, guitarist, music producer, and activist. Recognized early in her career for her social criticism and strong solidarity with the working class, Selda continues to be a fierce political voice.

Vera

Maths can be beautiful

Age: 10

My home:
I live with my mom, my dad, our two cats, Bisküvi and Lüpin, and our pet turtle, Yasef. We speak Turkish at home. My bedroom is just mine. I love changing its layout, decorating its walls, and making it feel like me.

My city:
Istanbul is famous for the Bosphorus Strait that connects the two continents of Asia and Europe, and its rich cultural diversity. My area is famous for its street cats; there's at least one in every street! Community matters here. You often see women in our street chatting from one window to another. I enjoy watching them, but sometimes I prefer to be alone with my thoughts.

¶ **I walk to school under the fig and plum trees.** Sometimes, I climb the trees to pick the fruit in spring. I feel like I'm wandering through a tiny forest. My school has a beautiful view of the Bosphorus. The building used to be an old Ottoman mansion. My grandma picks me up after school. Sometimes, we take an ice cream down to the seaside to watch the ships passing by.

¶ **I have been taking weekly Go classes since I was six.** Go is a traditional Japanese board game. I have competed in national and international tournaments. My teacher once said, "Chess is a struggle against your opponent, but Go is a struggle against yourself" – I agree!

¶ **I'm learning robotics and coding.** Creating your very own game is so exciting. Thinking that others might enjoy the game you've made is even better. I love to create things in general and have a 3D printer in my room. I always have a stash of boxes ready to make things with. I can build a little castle for myself, then tear it down and rebuild it into houses for my cats!

¶ **A headband is the most important part of any outfit.** I have a whole collection in different colours and styles. Sometimes, when I forget to wear one, my friends ask, "Where's your headband?" For me, headbands *are* Vera!

"*Most things relate back to maths. Even when I learn just a little, I notice it makes my life easier.*"

¶ **Two artist friends of my parents are teaching me to paint.** I lose track of time in the studio. I don't just paint with paint and paper; sometimes, I even use leaves to make collages. There are many artists in my area because of its history and natural beauty. I love to visit galleries in our neighbourhood to see their work.

UK

England, Scotland, and Wales share the island of Great Britain. Together with Northern Ireland across the Irish Sea, they form the United Kingdom (the UK). The UK's rich history is everywhere you look: Celtic and Roman ruins, medieval castles, country houses, royal palaces, and some of the first industrial buildings scatter the landscape. There are lots of cultural influences from all over the world here, because England, and then Britain, has a long history of colonizing other countries, a history the country is still coming to terms with.

Natural Beauty

The UK has a varied landscape. Southern England is lower lying, with woodlands and wildflower meadows. The Lake District in the north, the Scottish Highlands, and Snowdonia in Wales boast high peaks and mountain lakes. The dramatic arches rising from the sea of England's Jurassic Coast and the mystical basalt columns of Northern Ireland's Giant's Causeway are spectacular rock formations.

Did you know?
The Welsh dragon always faces left as though it is charging into battle, to symbolize bravery.

FAST FACTS

Official Name: United Kingdom of Great Britain and Northern Ireland

Home Nations: England, Northern Ireland, Scotland, Wales

Capital: London

Location: Northwestern Europe

Official Languages: English, Irish, Welsh, Scots Gaelic

Currency: Pound Sterling

Population: 69.2 million

Area: 243,610 km²

Beloved Characters

British authors have created some of the world's most beloved characters. Roald Dahl, Beatrix Potter, and Julia Donaldson have inspired generations of children with their stories. Famous bears Winnie the Pooh and Paddington were both created here, as well as the magical worlds of Peter Pan, Narnia, and, of course, Harry Potter.

The Jacobite steam train in Scotland was used as the *Hogwarts Express* in the Harry Potter films.

Celtic Britain

In around 1000 BCE, tribes of people sailed the seas from continental Europe to what is today Britain and Ireland. Today, these people are known as Celts. They were adventurous, worshipped many Gods, and discovered how to use iron to build their society. Irish, Scots Gaelic, and Welsh are all Celtic languages. Though they have differences in pronunciation and vocabulary, they all originate from the Celtic people who first settled in Britain and Ireland.

Who Rules Where?

The four nations of the UK share an elected government, based in London. They also share a king or queen, who is the Head of State here, and in 15 other Commonwealth realms around the world. While England is home to the national government, Scotland, Wales, and Northern Ireland also have some rules that are only to do with their countries, as well as their own smaller governments.

LONDON

Breakfast Time!

You may have heard of a "Full English", but what about a Full Irish, Scottish, or Welsh? Each nation has its own twist on the classic cooked breakfast. All countries agree on bacon and eggs, but in England you might add baked beans, in Scotland, square sausage, in Northern Ireland, boxty (potato pancake), and in Wales, seaweed.

Unique Traditions

In Wales, St Dwynwen's Day on 25 January brings the custom of exchanging hand-carved "love" spoons; whereas in Scotland the same date is reserved for celebrating the life of poet Robert Burns with a special dinner and dancing. Bonfire Night in England on 5 November remembers Guy Fawkes' failed plot to blow up Parliament, and in Northern Ireland, bonfires mark the Celtic festival of Samhain at the end of October.

REBEL GiRLS OF THE UK

Leah Williamson OBE (b. 1997) is an English professional footballer who plays for Women's Super League club, Arsenal, and captains the England women's national team.

Paleontologist and fossil collector **Mary Anning** (b. 1799) loved walking by the sea. One day, she discovered the first ichthyosaur (fish-lizard) fossil, and her find became a key piece in the puzzle of evolution.

Avalon

My dog makes me happy!

Age: 8

My home:
I live with my mum, my dad, my brother, Marcellus (11), and my dog, Dolly. She is a Frenchton: a French bulldog and a Boston Terrier cross. She is a colour called brindle, which is black with brown bits. She is the best dog ever!

My city:
I live on the Isle of Dogs in East London; the peninsula at the bendiest bit of the River Thames. It is believed to be where Henry VIII used to let his dogs run around. Dolly likes to run around here, too! There are lots of dog-friendly parks and we've even taken her for a ride on the Thames Clipper boat.

Dogs are my favourite, but I love all animals. I went to the zoo for my eighth birthday and I fed some lemurs and held a snake and a tenrec. Tenrecs look like hedgehogs, but they are some of the oldest mammals on Earth. I would love to run a doggy daycare one day.

My favourite foods are sushi and juicy cucumbers! London is more famous for its fish and chips, which I do like but I pick off the batter. I take a packed lunch to school with sushi or ham sandwiches, but the ham has to be thin! I eat extra fast with my friends so we get more play time.

My friends and I like to play tag and skipping games. We bring in little things to school for each other, too. We all get a turn to choose something from our "surprise box", like a little squishy unicorn. My friend Cece and I like to make up stories. We write them down, draw the characters, and make little books that we can keep. Our latest one was about an evil chicken who loved cucumbers.

I am learning to play the piano and the guitar. I like art and I'm most proud of making a papier-mâché tiger head, which is on our wall at home. I do a theatre club every Saturday and we put on *Elf the Musical* in December.

I'm good at running. I ran a mini marathon in the summer for a hospice, which is where you get cared for if you are really ill. My grandad went to one. The run was difficult because it was so hot that day and my trainer fell off, but I was proud that I did it and I got a medal at the end.

"Serendipity means a happy chance. It's my new favourite word – I learned it at school."

Safaa

My family supports me

¶ I like going out to restaurants, and we eat all sorts of food at home. Dinner might be butter chicken curry with rice and chapati, spaghetti bolognese, chicken pasta, biryani, burgers, or pizza. I love fish and chips, with salt and vinegar. You can't beat crunchy batter and soft white fish – I like to dip my chips into gravy!

¶ I love celebrating Eid, the Muslim festival that marks the end of Ramadan (the ninth month of the Islamic calendar, when adults fast). We get lots of presents, we spend time with our families, we wear nice clothes, and we eat lots of yummy food like chicken legs, lamb biryani, and desserts! We wear traditional clothing for mosque, including a headdress.

¶ I collect snowglobes. We bring them back from holidays, and from days out as a family. My favourite one came from our family trip to Qatar in 2023. It has different buildings from Qatar in it, such as Fanar, which is a mosque with palm trees in front of it. It is my favourite because it was my best holiday yet, and my first long flight.

¶ We are a close family. We love to celebrate birthdays and our successes, like getting the golden jumper at school, which is for children who have worked super hard throughout the week. It makes me smile when my sister hugs me, and I love playing with her. She draws amazing pictures and she always makes me laugh! My grandmother makes the yummiest food.

¶ My friends and I love making bracelets, singing, and dancing together. We ride our bikes and scooters, or do jigsaw puzzles. I like playing and watching football, and I'm loving learning to swim. My football team is Liverpool, but I like wearing strips from different teams and countries, too.

Age: 8

My home:
I live with my mum, my dad, and my sister, Safia (6). We speak English and Gujarati at home. I have my own room, decorated in a black and white theme. I have a giant squishy toy in the shape of a sun called Bijan, who lives on my bed!

My town:
Blackburn is a large industrial town in the northwest of England, known for its textile history. We have lots of mosques, shops, and schools, as well as a football stadium where the Blackburn Rovers play! We have plenty of parks and are close to the beautiful Lancashire hills.

REBEL GIRL SUPERPOWER: HAVING A LOVING FAMILY

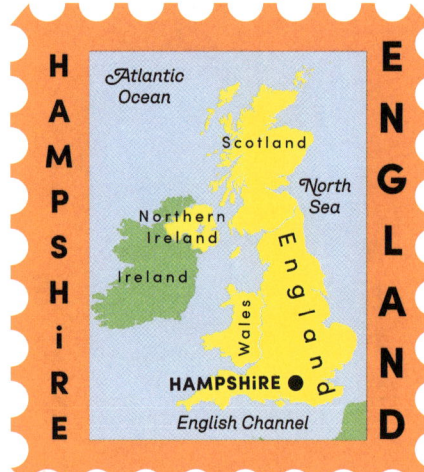

Millie

I love outdoor adventures

Age: 9

My home:
I live with my mum, my dad, my sister, Robyn (6), and our dogs, Rosie and Arlo. We live in a cottage in a little hamlet in the woods. It's in the South Downs National Park in Hampshire.

Our surroundings:
There are loads of deer, badgers, foxes, rabbits, and squirrels here, which we spot on our way to school. We sometimes hear owls and woodpeckers, too. We don't have street lights so we see lots of stars, and the planets are super bright at night. I love looking out for shooting stars and comets.

Ours is a strong community. We live next to our village hall where we have all sorts of celebrations, like Christmas drinks and a Harvest Festival celebration. At Halloween, we make the hall look like a haunted house and we go trick-or-treating up the lane with flaming torches. We have an annual Easter egg hunt, too!

We have forest school on Wednesdays. We get to spend the morning in the woods. The stream that we play in has mud and clay at the side of it that you can make things with. When we use sticks to make bows and arrows, or leaves to make crowns, it feels like we are in the Stone Age.

I had an operation on my eye when I was four. The operation was two hours long and I had to wear a hospital gown. I had to be super brave because they put me to sleep for the operation. Afterwards, I had to wear a bandage for a few days but I was absolutely fine!

Arlene Burns is an adventurer who inspires me. She does amazing things, like climbing volcanoes and going down a Tibetan river. She was the first woman to become a white-water river guide in New Zealand.

I don't eat meat because I love animals so much. They are my best friends. As well as having our two dogs, we share chickens with our neighbours. We feed them and collect their eggs. I love picking one of them up and stroking her.

My friends and I like to ride on our hoverboards. We also play on our bikes and skateboards in front of the house. It's really fun near us when it snows. We go sledging on the giant hills. I even tried out Mum's snowboard!

"It's my dream to travel the world as an explorer or a scientist."

Sidney

I love helping good causes

My grandparents come from the Caribbean, and we sometimes speak an Anglophone Creole as a family as well as English. We mostly cook Caribbean food at home, too. I especially love to eat plantain.

I'm on my school council this year. I am part of my school's eco community, too. I would love to design and build environmentally friendly buildings around the world when I'm older.

I'm proud of organizing a sponsored roller-skate, raising more than £1,000 for charity. I arranged for lots of companies to donate money, and I even had my own kit printed displaying all their logos. One sports shop donated new skates! I was meant to skate 10 kilometres but I managed 11 kilometres in total in the end.

We love to go down to Kent for holidays, where my family has a caravan. I sometimes take my friends and we bring our bikes and roller-skates to explore on.

In my spare time, I play the violin and I love baking. I'm a self-taught gymnast, and I like basketball, football, and swimming, too. I especially love spending time with my 10-year-old triplet cousins, Sofia, Federica, and Olivia. They only live 30 minutes away and are so fun.

I really love fashion. At the moment I like wearing tracksuits and flares, but for special occasions I prefer to wear pretty dresses.

Age: 8

My home:
I live with my mum, my dad, my big sister, Izzy (25), Summer the tabby cat, and our new cockapoo puppy, Ruby. I got to choose the paint colour when we decorated my room during the summer holidays. I chose yellow! It's well organized and my favourite thing in it is my TV bed.

My city:
I love that East London is so multicultural. There are lots of things to do here, and most of my friends live close by. We mostly walk and cycle everywhere, but occasionally we drive instead.

REBEL GIRL SUPERPOWER: RAISING MONEY FOR CHARITY

René

Call us Bean...

Age: 10

Our city:
Glasgow is the biggest city in Scotland. "Glasgow" means "green glen" or "green hollow" in Gaelic, and it has plenty of leafy parks. It is a city of art and culture as well as sport; the rivalry between its two football clubs, Rangers and Celtic, is world famous!

My favourite thing to wear is my football strip. I absolutely love football. I play it a lot, and I want to be a professional footballer when I grow up. I also play a bit of tennis and hockey. Even though my favourite sport to play is definitely football, my favourite sport to watch is tennis.

We lived in Spain for three months of last year, and we went to a Spanish school. It was great fun and we made lots of new friends. We sometimes speak Spanish at home even now we're back, so we can practise what we learned.

Playing the piano in my spare time makes me happy. I also play the trumpet at school. I attend my school's gaming club at lunchtime – we meet to play games on our consoles. I love games in general, and I can solve a Rubik's Pyramid Cube in seven seconds!

I like making bracelets with my friends, or bouncing on our sunken trampoline. We also enjoy doing arts and crafts, especially painting. I love to read, and my favourite types of books are probably mystery and comedy books.

"Although our dog Rosie is old, she is as cheeky as a wee puppy!"

Matilda

and Tilda

REBEL GiRL SUPERPOWER
OUR TALENT FOR FOOTBALL

"Rosie cheers me up whenever I am sad."

Our home:
We live with our mum, dad, brother, Peadar (24), and our beloved cockapoo, Rosie! We also have another brother, Hamish (27), and two sisters, Iona and Niamh (21). They are twins like us! René and I share a room. It is very colourful, with plenty of toys and books in it.

Playing football makes me really happy, it calms me down if I am annoyed. I play on our school team, and for two teams outside of school. I also play tennis outside of school, and hockey for the school team.

My favourite part of school is seeing my friends. We get to chat before school and at break times, and we hang out and play games on the equipment. I love PE, and my teachers make maths really fun, too – we play lots of maths games, like Countdown. I really enjoy baking in Food Technology. I like making Scottish Tablet, which is a bit like fudge, but sweeter and a lot tastier.

I'm proud of how much I have improved at reading. I used to find it difficult, but now I have special coloured glasses to help me. I read a lot more books than I used to, and school is much easier now. I especially love Tom Fletcher's books.

Two women who inspire me are Sam Kerr, an Australian footballer who promotes girls' football, and Brogan Hay, who plays in the Scotland women's football team, just like I would like to one day.

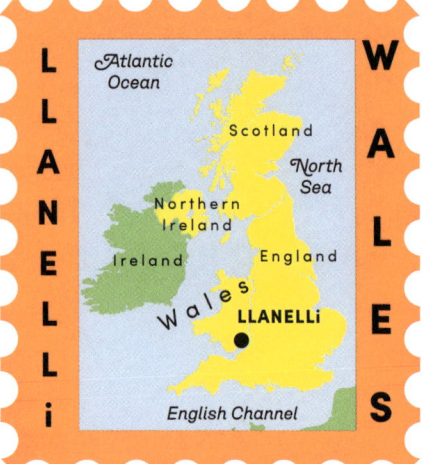

Age: **10**

My home:
I live with my mum, my dad, and my sister, Winter (5). I have my own room, with a *Minecraft* tree painted on the wall, and *Minecraft* curtains. I have a big bed, and a desk for drawing and writing. I have lots of notebooks hidden everywhere with my stories in them, and lots and lots of soft toys.

My town:
I live in Llanelli (it's pronounced "thluh·NETH·lee"). It's quite a small coastal market town near Swansea, in southwestern Wales. We speak English and Welsh here. We have a famous rugby team called the Llanelli Scarlets and beautiful beaches nearby, framed by green fields and rolling hills.

Leela

I love video games

I am vegetarian. I usually have cereal for breakfast, but sometimes Mum makes me pancakes, or Dad brings me pastries home from the hotel he works at. I have school dinners for lunch, unless it's something I don't like, then Mum makes me a packed lunch. I really like Welsh cakes (a cross between a scone and a pancake), especially the kind with chocolate chips.

I play a lot of *Minecraft* with my friends, and I enjoy watching commentary videos on YouTube. I could tell you absolutely everything about the game, *The Legend of Zelda*. I love it. My favourite T-shirt has Zelda on it, and we even had a tabby cat named after her! She lived until she was 13. I miss her and our other tabby, Joey, very much.

School is different every day for me. Sometimes it can be stressful and loud, and we have to do difficult maths; other days it can be chill and we get "golden time" to play on the computer. I love it when I get to play a game I made up with my friends called "Legendary". We all have different powers and we turn into animals. We have new names in the game. We play in teams, or we work together to build the story.

I go to a performing arts group on Saturdays. It is close enough to walk from my house. I am playing Lavender in a production of *Matilda* in a few months. I'm really looking forward to it! I'm taking trumpet lessons at school, too.

I love fantasy books and anime. I'm inspired by the character Rayla from *The Dragon Prince*. She's very skilled at fighting, she's a good climber, and – most importantly – a good friend. My auntie is teaching me archery so I can be just like Rayla. She used to be an archery teacher and she gave me a wooden bow and arrow. I love to watch fencing, too.

NORTH AMERICA

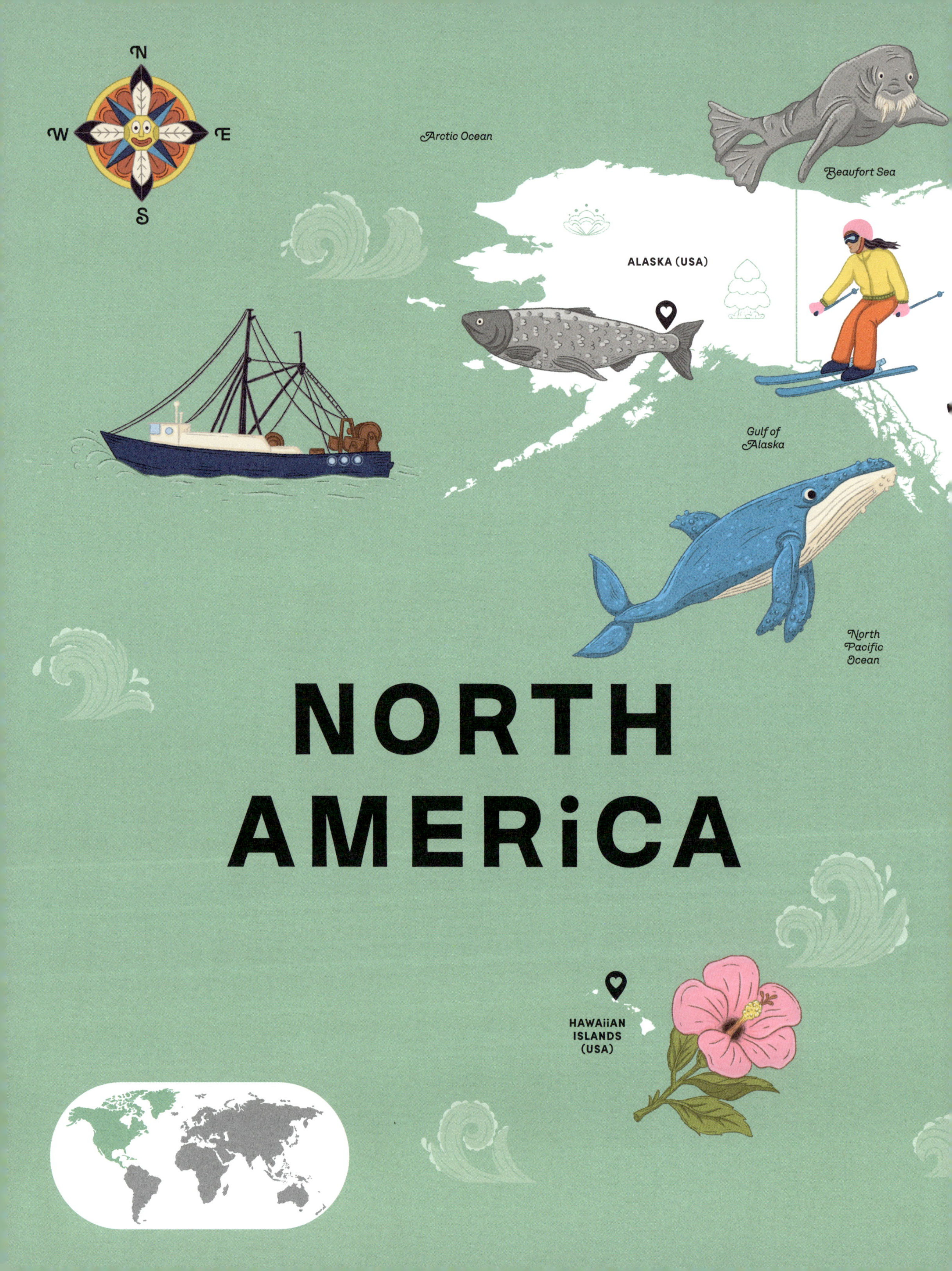
N
S
W
E
Arctic Ocean
Beaufort Sea
ALASKA (USA)
Gulf of Alaska
North Pacific Ocean
HAWAiiAN ISLANDS (USA)

Canada

Imagine how large a country has to be to span six different time zones! Canada is the second-biggest country in the world after Russia, stretching for around 7,500 kilometres from east to west. It also has a longer coastline and more lakes than anywhere else on the planet – nearly two million of them. Towering mountains, vast green forests, and a varied climate makes it a haven for nature lovers – as well as for the three species of bear that are found in the wild here.

Canada's Climate

There is often as much as a 30°C difference in average temperature between the north and the south of this enormous country. Thanks to icy, treeless Arctic tundra in the north, the freezing interior plains in the middle, and the snowy Rocky Mountains in the west, Canada's average daily temperature is the lowest in the world. But it is not always cold! Summers can be warm and humid.

Land of Languages

French and British colonizers came to Canada in the 16th and 17th centuries, bringing their languages with them. While English and French are the official languages of the country, there are more than 70 different Indigenous languages spoken by First Nations people, Métis, and Inuit in Canada.

Wildlife Wonders

From bears to sea otters, there is a host of incredible wildlife to be found in Canada. The national animal is the beaver, and you can find these busy creatures building dams in rivers and streams across the country. You might also see moose, wolves, caribou, and bison – not to mention bald eagles flying overhead.

FAST FACTS

Capital: Ottawa

Location: North America

Official Languages: English, French

Border Countries: USA

Currency: Canadian Dollar

Population: 41.29 million

Area: 9.985 million km²

Incredible Inuksuks

Across the Arctic region of Canada are unique stone structures known as *inuksuks*. The Inuit and other Arctic peoples have created *inuksuks* for many generations, and for lots of different reasons. Some mark sacred places, others indicate good fishing or hunting spots, and some are signposts for travellers. On Baffin Island, there are around 100 *inuksuks* at Inuksuk Point, with some thought to be around two thousand years old.

Did you know? Canada has the most doughnut shops per capita in the world!

Life on the Ice

Ice hockey – simply known as "hockey" in Canada – is the official national winter sport and a popular pastime for all ages. Canadians often start learning to skate as young as three! Lacrosse (a team sport where players use sticks with nets at the end to shoot a rubber ball into the opponent's goal) is the official national summer sport.

"Sugaring Off"

Canada is rich in natural resources, such as oil and gas, but perhaps its most famous export is maple syrup! Canada produces about 80 per cent of the world's supply of pure maple syrup. "Sugaring off" is a special time in March and April, when the sap is harvested from maple trees then boiled to produce syrup. It marks the end of a long, cold winter and the fresh start that spring brings.

The Mounties

The Royal Canadian Mounted Police, also known as the "Mounties", is the national police service. On ceremonial occasions, Mounties wear distinctive red uniforms, and some ride horses. Aspiring RCMP cadets go through a very intense 26-week training programme that includes outdoor exercises in sub-zero temperatures!

REBEL GiRLS OF CANADA

Advocating for people's right to clean water, and the rights of water itself, **Autumn Peltier** (b. 2004) is an Indigenous activist from the Wiikwemkoong First Nation on Manitoulin Island, Ontario.

Prizewinning author **Margaret Atwood** (b. 1939) grew up in the woods of Ottawa, where she loved all things wild. Her thought-provoking books encourage people to consider the state of the world we live in.

Maya

I love to put thoughts into words

Age: 13

My home:
I live with my mom and dad. We speak both English and French at home. In my room, I have a desk covered in books, a guitar, two ukuleles, a magnet board, and an LP record player.

My town:
Cochrane is a small town in northeastern Ontario. We have a skating rink, a bowling alley, a cinema, a beach, a pool, and the Polar Bear Habitat – a facility dedicated to caring for our two polar bears, Ganuk and Henry. It's the only one of its kind in the world! We have amazing snowmobile, ski, and snowshoe trails in winter.

¶ I'm French Canadian. It's ironic that I'm vegan because many of our traditional foods are meat based. I love *marie fendue*, a type of fried bread dough my mammy makes when my cousins come over; we dip it in molasses – delicious!

¶ I love to read young adult fiction. My favourite genres are sci-fi, speculative fiction, and fantasy. I write my own short stories, too. I like imagining alternate universes and creating characters so that the story unfolds before me. My characters decide their own fate. My dream job is to be a writer or a lawyer – or even both!

¶ My music studies are very important to me. I take piano lessons, play the flute in my school band, and love playing the guitar and ukulele. I write my own songs, and have attended two residential music camps.

¶ Travelling with my family is always fun. We go on city breaks to Toronto or Ottawa, or we take camping trips to provincial parks. We go to "Rock on the River" in Timmins in the summer. It's a three-day festival of rock and country music. They have events for families in the day before the main acts perform at night.

¶ I'm part of the volleyball programme at school, and I like cross-country skiing and skating. My friends and I enjoy swimming, or playing pool in my basement. We play a lot of singing and clapping games, and of course we practise songs on our ukuleles.

¶ My neighbour's dog is like family to me! Her name is Rosette and she only understands French. I taught her to high five and shake paws. She's so cute.

REBEL GiRL SUPERPOWER
MY WRITING

Aiva

I'm passionate about our planet

¶ I'm Canadian-Italian so I really love pasta dishes, and my grandmother's Sunday sauce! Montreal is known for our famous *poutine* dish: french fries topped with gravy and cheese curds. It is definitely a must-try! We are a very multi-cultural city, and it's great to see how many different ethnicities and their influences you will find here.

¶ I love International Women's History Month in March. My mom, sister, and I read a different story about women who have changed history every day. It's so empowering. I am also part of my mom's *FearlesslyKind Girl* mentorship programme. She hosts empowerment workshops for tween and teen girls. I love to dance with them and just hang out!

¶ My dream is to be an environmentalist – or anything to do with making the planet a safer, better place to live. I'm so passionate about the environment that I reached out to mentors at the Jane Goodall Institute to help me write and record a TED-Ed talk called *"Little Pollution = Big Problem"*, about the growing climate crisis. I am proud to be raising awareness.

¶ I enjoy taking boxing lessons, and I like playing basketball and skateboarding. I love watching football on TV with my family every time there's a World Cup. We all support Italy!

¶ My bookcase is bursting with books, from the *Nancy Drew* series and Raina Telgemeier's books, to the *Babysitters Club* series and many girls' empowerment books. I read a lot, and I enjoy writing stories.

¶ Helping with cleaning is one of my chores at home, along with setting the table for dinner, and folding and putting away my laundry.

Age: 11

My home:
I live with my mom, dad, and sister, Emmi (8). We speak English at home. I have my own room, and my favourite things in it will always be my books, and my favourite little reindeer stuffy.

My city:
Montréal is a big city on an island. It has lots of beautiful parks and a big mountain called Mount Royal. It is a bilingual city: all our signs are in both English and French!

"I am inspired by Jane Goodall and my mother. They are my role models and I look up to them a lot."

The Caribbean

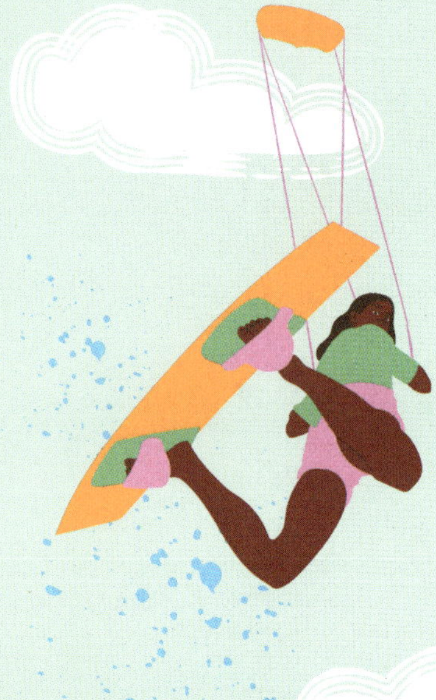

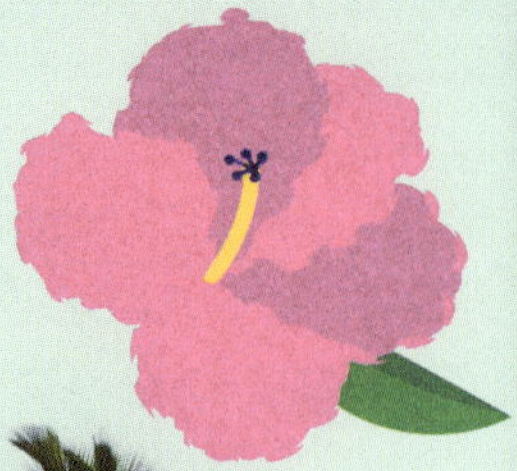

The region known as the Caribbean is made up of more than 7,000 islands, including 13 independent island countries and some territories governed by other nations. The islands are grouped: the Greater Antilles, which includes larger islands like Cuba; the Lucayan Archipelago, also known as the Bahamas; and the Lesser Antilles, which has smaller islands like Aruba. It's a large geographical area made up of many unique cultures and identities, but the islands within it also share a history shaped by colonization and slavery.

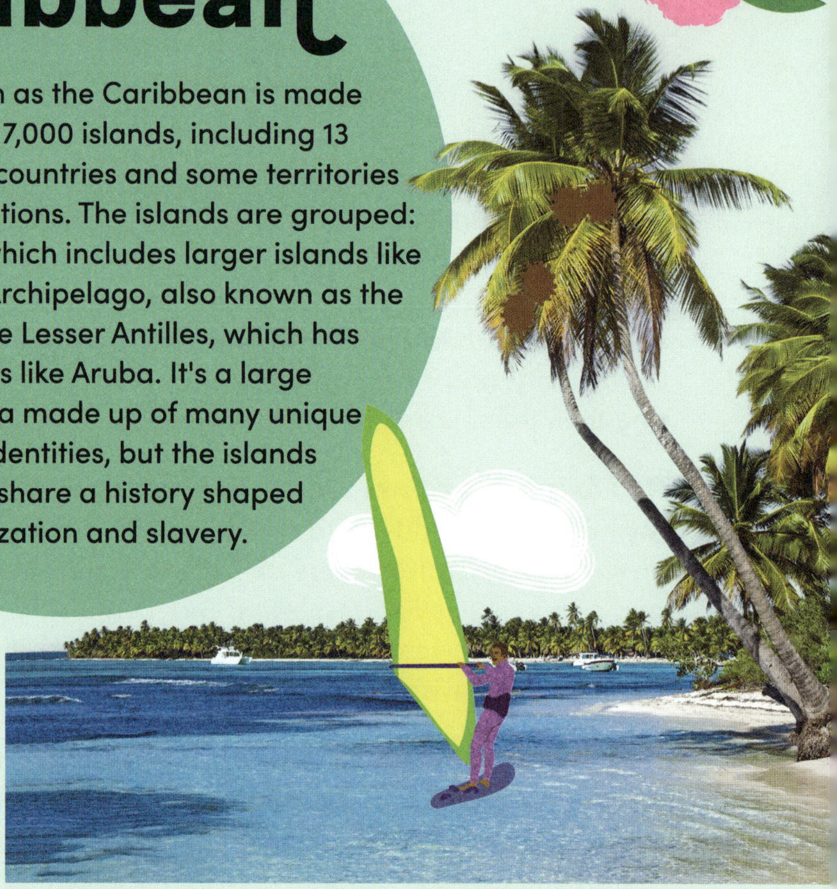

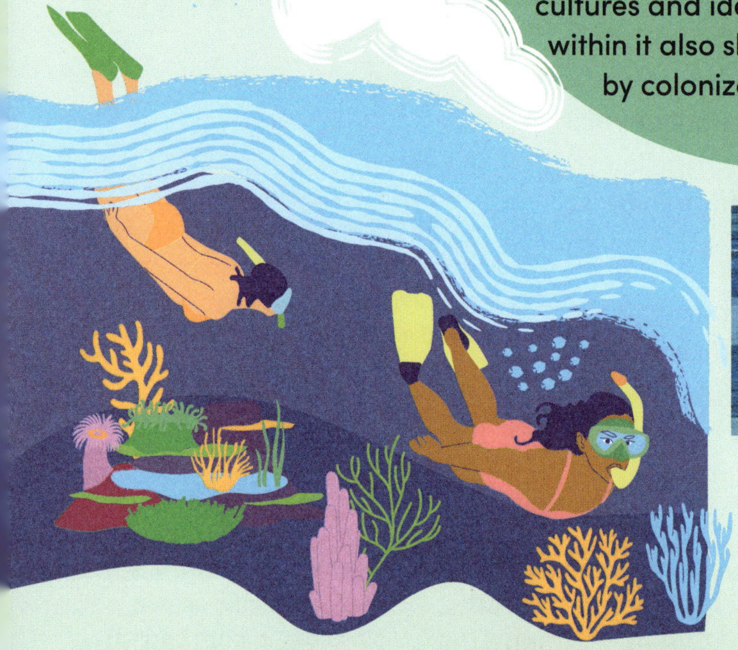

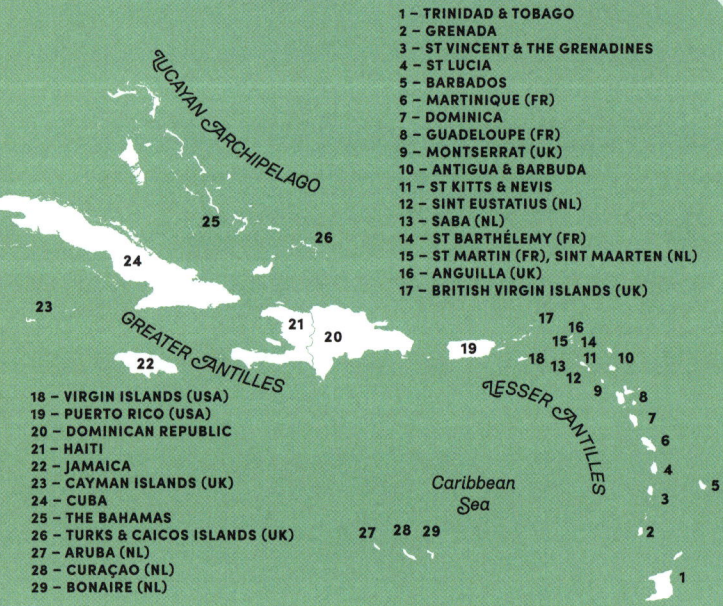

1 – TRINIDAD & TOBAGO
2 – GRENADA
3 – ST VINCENT & THE GRENADINES
4 – ST LUCIA
5 – BARBADOS
6 – MARTINIQUE (FR)
7 – DOMINICA
8 – GUADELOUPE (FR)
9 – MONTSERRAT (UK)
10 – ANTIGUA & BARBUDA
11 – ST KITTS & NEVIS
12 – SINT EUSTATIUS (NL)
13 – SABA (NL)
14 – ST BARTHÉLEMY (FR)
15 – ST MARTIN (FR), SINT MAARTEN (NL)
16 – ANGUILLA (UK)
17 – BRITISH VIRGIN ISLANDS (UK)
LUCAYAN ARCHIPELAGO
GREATER ANTILLES
LESSER ANTILLES
Caribbean Sea
18 – VIRGIN ISLANDS (USA)
19 – PUERTO RICO (USA)
20 – DOMINICAN REPUBLIC
21 – HAITI
22 – JAMAICA
23 – CAYMAN ISLANDS (UK)
24 – CUBA
25 – THE BAHAMAS
26 – TURKS & CAICOS ISLANDS (UK)
27 – ARUBA (NL)
28 – CURAÇAO (NL)
29 – BONAIRE (NL)

STEM in the Caribbean

The Caribbean Science Foundation (CSF) provides young Caribbean STEM enthusiasts with opportunities to grow their passion. Kids can take part in robotics camps, coding workshops, and even compete in the Caribbean STEM Olympiads. Older high-school students can apply to attend a 5-week STEM summer programme, where they can learn the skills they need to go on to higher study and build successful careers in STEM subjects.

Colonial Past

The Caribbean has a complicated history. European colonizers arrived in 1492 and brought with them diseases that wiped out most of the Indigenous peoples of the region, including the Carib and Arawak groups of people. Europeans abducted African people from their homelands, enslaved them, and brought them to Caribbean islands to labour under terrible conditions on sugar, tobacco, and cotton plantations. Slavery lasted for hundreds of years before it was outlawed in the 1800s. The Caribbean today is impacted by the legacies of centuries of exploitation, but it also reflects the strength and resilience of those who lived through it, and their descendants, who continue to celebrate their heritages and emancipation.

Beautiful Barbados

Archaeologists believe that Barbados has been inhabited by humans for 4,000 years, and today it is the most densely populated island in the Caribbean. It was one of the first islands to be colonized by Europeans, at which time many important sites and artefacts from its past were destroyed. Barbadian culture is a unique blend of West African and British influences, but today, Barbados is an independent country, and its capital, Bridgetown, is its largest city. The island is known for its music, like soca, calypso, reggae, and the folk tuk band music.

BRiDGETOWN

Hurricane Alley

Much of the Caribbean is in "Hurricane Alley", an area of the Atlantic where strong winds, warm seas, and high humidity combine to super-charge storms moving towards the islands. Hurricanes often hit between May and October each year. These storms bring torrential rain, violent winds, and sometimes cause floods or damage. People living in the impacted area prepare by keeping an eye on weather warnings, gathering supplies, and taking shelter.

Did you know? The Caribbean has two distinct seasons. The dry season and the wet season split the year in half.

British Virgin Islands (BVI)

This group of 60 islands is home to just over 30,000 people. Colonized by different European nations over centuries, it also has a past steeped in stories of pirates and shipwrecks. On Norman Island, said to be the inspiration for *Treasure Island*, there are huge caves where pirates likely hid out and stowed their plundered loot. Sailing is the biggest sport in the BVI, and the largest event is the Spring Regatta, a series of races held in April. Captains and their crews on boats of all sizes come from all around the world to attend. Since 2009, the BVI has also made a name for itself hosting international basketball events.

Did you know? Each island has its own language, traditions, and heroes—no two are the same

Caribbean Cricket

The sport of cricket is part of the culture on many islands. It was originally brought to the Caribbean by the British, and played on the islands they colonized. Now, top cricketers come together from across multiple Caribbean islands to play as one unified team in international tournaments. The team is known as Cricket West Indies, or, more affectionately by cricket fans as the "Windies". At the Women's T20 Cricket World Cup in 2024, the Windies Women made it to the semi-finals.

REBEL GiRLS OF CARiBBEAN

Puerta Rican scientist **Wanda Díaz-Merced** (b. c. 1982) lost her sight while at university. She pursued studies in astrophysics and went on to work for NASA, where she analyses radio data by listening.

Nanny of the Maroons (b. c. 1685, Ghana), was an early 18th-century freedom fighter and leader of the Jamaican Maroons. She led a community of escaped enslaved people, and is still celebrated today.

"I prefer silks and cottons in earth tones, or light shades of pink."

Faith

I have a passion for fashion!

On special occasions, I like to eat fried flying fish. I eat it with *cou cou* (cooked cornmeal mixed with okra and water). Day to day, I typically eat simpler food, such as vegetables, fruit, rice, or pasta, but I really like to try new things on weekends, like sushi or Chinese food.

I love watching the annual Crop Over celebrations. Thousands of people dress in brightly coloured costumes to dance behind carnival floats on the first Monday in August. We take the day off work and school to toast the end of the crop season. The sugar cane that we grow here is so vital for the island. It is harvested to make sugar for export as well as for local consumption.

My friends and I enjoy going to the movies together. We also have sleepovers and visit farmers' markets! I love baking in my spare time, too. I make brownies, cookies, cakes, and cupcakes of all flavours. I also like to read non-fiction books full of facts. My favourites are the *Guinness World Record* books, and books about genealogy.

I want to be a lawyer or a fashion marketer: a lawyer because I'm inspired by Michelle Obama, and a fashion marketer because I love clothes. I especially like to wear dresses. I enjoy accessorizing them with handbags and jewellery that I buy online or on shopping trips with my friends. We love to visit pop-up shops where there is a lot of variety. I'm interested in interior design, too.

I have recently joined the Girl Guides. I love the social aspect of it since we get to mix with girls from other schools. I have only been at my school for a year, so Girl Guiding is a good chance to make new friends.

Age: **13**

My home:
I live with my mother and our dog, Spark, in a two-story house with a nice, grassy backyard. Spark is a Canadian Presa mixed with a Rottweiler. She is brown and very active. I have my own bedroom. The walls are hand painted with animals from the African savanna. Air conditioning keeps me cool in our hot climate!

My city:
I live in a very peaceful neighbourhood where everyone is very friendly. Saint Philip is at the easternmost tip of the island of Barbados. It is well-known for calypso music. Some of the world's best calypsonians and performers come from here.

REBEL GIRL SUPERPOWER
MY ABILITY TO SENSE OTHER PEOPLE'S EMOTIONS

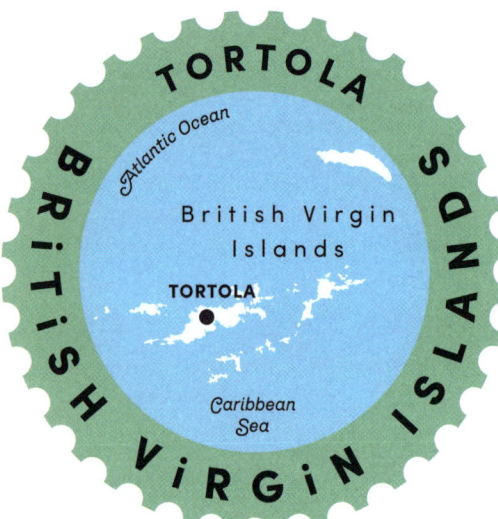

Aerin

I'm happiest in the ocean

Age: **13**

My home:
I live with my mum, my dad, our three dogs, Indie, Widget, and Piper, and a cat named Stella! I am lucky enough to have my own room and the theme is beach coastal. I am an only child so I often feel lonely – my pets always sleep on my bed.

My city:
I live on Tortola, an island that is 19 kilometres long and only 5 kilometres wide, in the Caribbean. We are surrounded by the most beautiful crystal-clear water. Where I live is full of natural wonders created by previous volcanic activity.

"I'm very passionate about competition, the art of challenge, and pushing myself to become better."

School starts at 7:45am and ends at 3pm. We do seven subjects every day, for 50 minutes each, with a lunch break in the middle. Outside of school, I spend most of my free time either playing football (for my school, local women's league, and national team), or sailing. I used to play the steel pan, too, but I gave up!

I have a group of about eight girl friends, some of whom go to my school, but the rest I know through football and sailing. When we're not sailing or playing football, we like to surf, swim, have sleepovers, go snorkelling, diving, hiking, and just being goofy together.

My ambition is to be a boat captain when I grow up. I just got back from representing the British Virgin Islands in a sailing competition against lots of competitors from other Caribbean islands. I want to sail around the world just like Jessica Watson, the Australian who achieved the youngest solo circumnavigation. She is so inspiring.

I love that in the Caribbean we have *Mocca Jumbies* (dancers on stilts in bright costumes). Another lovely Caribbean tradition is that it is very important to greet people. If you walk into a room or shop it is customary to say, "good morning" or "good afternoon", even if you don't know anyone there.

We have three pet dogs. They are all female, and are all rescue dogs that we've found around the island. I love them dearly. Two are quite old and grey, and we still take them to the beach. Our youngest, Piper, loves to sleep in my bed. We adopted my cat, Stella, from our local animal shelter about six years ago. She is a very petite calico cat and is best friends with Piper.

The USA

The USA has the world's largest economy, which is boosted by a strong culture of entrepreneurship; plentiful natural resources, such as oil and gas; and renewables, such as solar and wind power. Its land is divided into 50 states, each with its own identity, landscape, and traditions. The USA's many cultures and climate zones are so varied that it can seem like multiple countries rolled into one, but its national identity is strong. Its powerful influence can be felt across the globe – from food to tech, to music and movies.

THE FiRST AEROPLANE

Leading the Way

The USA is known for its world-changing innovations in science and technology. The invention of the aeroplane by the Wright brothers in 1903 forever changed how people travel. NASA, the US space agency, made history by landing the first astronauts on the Moon in 1969. Top US technology companies such as Apple and Google have revolutionized how people across the globe use technology and communicate.

Famous Cities

Cities like New York, Los Angeles, and Washington, D.C. are famous all over the world and can be seen in countless movies and TV shows. New York City is known for its busy streets, tall skyscrapers, and the Statue of Liberty, while Los Angeles is the heart of the Hollywood movie industry. Washington, D.C. is home to the country's government, and also to important landmarks like the White House and the Lincoln Memorial.

FAST FACTS

Official Name: United States of America

Official Language: English

Capital: Washington, D.C.

Currency: US Dollar

Location: North America

Population: 340.1 million

Border Countries: Canada, Mexico

Area: 9.834 million km²

NEW YORK

THE GRAND CANYON

Fast Food
People from all around the world have come to live in the USA, bringing their traditions, food, and cultures with them. As a result, you can find almost any cuisine you want in US cities. The USA's fast-food culture has been adopted by many countries across the world too, where food is served at drive-through restaurants.

Big and Beautiful
The USA is the third-largest country in the world by area, and is home to a wide range of ecosystems, from temperate forests to deserts. Its giant sequoias are the tallest trees on earth, with some reaching over 90 metres and living for thousands of years. The Grand Canyon in Arizona, the Everglades in Florida, and the Great Lakes region are just some of the natural wonders to visit in this incredible country.

Did you know? The Great Lakes contain one-fifth of Earth's fresh water!

Fighting for Equality
The Civil Rights Movement in the 1950s and 1960s was a fight for equality for Black Americans, who faced segregation – being separated from white people in places like schools, buses, and restaurants. Rosa Parks became a symbol of resistance when she refused to give up her bus seat in 1955. Martin Luther King Jr played a key role, leading peaceful protests and inspiring many with his famous *"I Have a Dream"* speech. Their efforts led to segregation becoming illegal, but the fight for racial equality in the USA still continues today.

Power of Powwows
Powwows are fun but also sacred occasions where Indigenous peoples gather together across the USA to honour and demonstrate their different nations' cultures and traditions. Participants in powwows wear regalia, which is often created from treasured family heirlooms. Feathers in regalia are particularly precious and sacred. There is always drumming, singing, and dancing at a powwow. Some dances might be for celebration or for memorial reasons, and are sometimes performed competitively in front of audiences. There are also social dances where everyone is encouraged to join in!

REBEL GIRLS OF THE USA

Katherine Johnson (b. 1918) overcame racial and gender discrimination to become a top NASA mathematician. Her work helped to send astronauts to the moon.

Taylor Swift (b. 1989) is a music icon, self-made billionaire, and songwriter. Chronicling her life and loves through her passion for musical storytelling, Taylor has become a household name no one will forget.

"I think extraterrestrial life exists, and want to prove to everyone that it does!"

Ruhee

I'm a good listener

My family speaks Marathi and English at home.
Marathi is an Indian dialect, and I have been learning Hindi as well, so I can enjoy Bollywood movies! My mom prepares a lot of Marathi food, which includes my favourite dish, *pav bhaji* – a soft, puffy bread served with lentils and vegetables.

We host a Diwali firework celebration every year for some of our friends. I especially like this time because we invite our non-Hindu friends too. They are able to enjoy Diwali without all of the religious traditions. For some of the Indian festivals we celebrate, I like to wear my traditional *salwar kurta*. Otherwise I wear dresses with my favourite red bow.

I am most proud of my small face-painting business. I took an after-school class to learn how to start a small business. I made over 50 dollars in less than two hours at my first event! After subtracting my costs, I ended up with 40 dollars, and donated this amount to UNICEF.

I want to be a lawyer when I grow up, and then work my way up to my dream job: a supreme court justice like my idol, Ruth Bader Ginsburg.

I feel like nothing can go wrong when I'm reading. I prefer to read books that I can relate to, like the *Mr. Terupt* series by Rob Buyea. I also like graphic novels, because I like looking at the drawing styles and experimenting with my own sketches. I like to write poetry, too.

Hula-hooping with my friends is so much fun. My record is one hour and 14 minutes straight! If we're not feeling active, we just like to talk and play hand games. I play clarinet in the advanced band at school, and I also sing in the chorus.

Age: 10

My home:
I live with my mom, my dad, and my little brother, Yash (6). I share a room with my brother. We have an entire wall decorated with polka-dot stickers and a beautiful dreamcatcher hung high up next to our closet. I have a small, standing desk next to a white bookshelf that holds some of my favourite reads.

My town:
Livingston is a pleasant town in New Jersey with beautiful colours in the fall. It has a pool, a vast library, lots of playgrounds, and many hiking trails. Livingston has a rich history. It is named after William Livingston, a key figure both as a Founding Father of the United States and of New Jersey. I'm proud to call this place home.

REBEL GIRL SUPERPOWER: MY FRIENDS CAN ALWAYS COME TO ME

Beatriz

I want to keep exploring

Age: 9

My home:
I live with my mom, my dad, my brothers, Felix (6) and Joaquin (1), and my sister, Marisol (3). We have a funny-looking dog, Fry, and a pet jumping spider, Lucas. I share a room with my siblings. In my culture, it's normal for families to sleep in the same room. Our room is decorated simply. It is painted orange because I was born in the fall.

My city:
I live in Chicago. We live right across the street from a forest preserve that the Chicago River runs through. I like being able to live in a big city with lots of culture, sports, restaurants, stores, and excitement, but also having access to the beauty of nature. People don't always expect that from Chicago.

"I like to wear colours like purple and blue because they make me feel strong and powerful."

My family is part Cuban and part Mexican; it is very important for us to speak Spanish as part of our culture. My school is dual language and we have a special curriculum that teaches us about the history of Latin America, as well as current issues our people are facing. My family is very supportive of my education.

I stay connected to my culture through dance, tradition, and advocacy. I take part in Danza Azteca to honour my Aztec heritage, and I also perform various *bailes folclóricos*, which are very beautiful dances. My favourite cultural tradition by far is *El Día del Niño* (Children's Day) in April, when we get to celebrate what it means to be a kid.

We celebrate Día de los Muertos (Day of the Dead). It's a Mexican festival honouring the people in our lives who have died. We create beautiful colourful *ofrendas* (altars) displaying pictures of the people who are no longer with us. We add sugar skulls called *calaveras* as well as little offerings of the things that the person loved in life, like sweets and ornaments. Beautiful orange marigolds make everything look super bright and joyful.

I am so passionate about science. It relates to absolutely everything. It's my dream to be an astronaut. I want to study the stars and black holes, and to travel in outer space to discover new things. Mae Jemison has roots in Chicago like me, and worked as an engineer, doctor, and astronaut. I admire her because she was the first African-American woman to go to space; I want to be the first person to do something amazing too.

School is a couple of blocks away from Wrigley Field, where the Chicago Cubs play baseball. The area is very lively if there's been a game on. I support the Cubs, but my mom supports the other Chicago team, the White Sox!

Charlotte

My nickname is Char Char

¶ I like to eat fast food and salads, but my favourite meal of the day is breakfast because I love chocolate-chip waffles so much. I usually wake up at 6:45am, when I get dressed, eat breakfast, and watch TV before school. Sometimes, if I have a test, my mom and I study in the car on the way.

¶ I have so much fun making slime with my friends. We make it at sleepovers and playdates. We make bracelets together, too. We're in a music group called Rock Shed where we play instruments, sing, and write music. I play the ukulele. We're making a music video soon! For sports, I play basketball and volleyball, and watch American football. When I'm alone, I crochet, draw, read graphic novels, and listen to music.

¶ I have a tortoise named Timmy. Taking care of him and his terrarium is one of my responsibilities at home. I also make my bed, and help with the dishes and the laundry. I had a dog named Kermit who died, and I miss him a lot. My mom said we can get a new dog next year.

¶ I haven't worked out what I want to be yet. It's a choice between a musician, an artist, a lawyer, and a nurse! I'm proud of being a daughter of a future nurse: my mom is training to be one right now. My me-maw (grandma), my mom, and my aunties are all inspiring women.

¶ My city is famous for the Civil Rights Movement. Four little girls died in the racist bombing of the 16th Street Baptist Church in 1963, and the public outrage afterwards helped to accelerate change. The Civil Rights Act of 1964 banned discrimination based on race, colour, religion, gender, or national origin in the United States.

¶ "Slay" is slang for looking really cute! I wear dresses and skirts for special occasions. If it's not a special occasion I wear trousers. I like to wear leggings and a sweatshirt, because I get chilly. I love to shop with Mom.

Age: 9

My home:
I live with my mom in a condo. My bedroom is purple with mermaid wallpaper, and I love my mini fridge, my bunk bed, and my en-suite bathroom! We have shared outdoor space with our neighbours. We are growing strawberries, peppers, tomatoes, aubergine, and okra this year in raised beds.

My town:
I live in a leafy suburb of Birmingham, Alabama, in the southeast of the United States. We have lots of cafés and restaurants, as well as Red Mountain Park, with hiking and biking trails, a zip-line course, and a rock climbing tower! Our neighbourhood is pretty. My friends are my neighbours. I love them!

Colette

My friends call me Coco

Age: 9

My home:
I live with my mom, my dad, my cat, my two dogs, and my brother, L.B., who is 16 months younger than me. He can be annoying because most younger brothers are. I used to share a room with him, but now I have my own room downstairs. It is decorated with lots of NFL (National Football League) decorations, keepsakes, and photos from camp.

My city:
Baton Rouge is famous for being the state capital of Louisiana and the seat of its government. It was built on the banks of the Mississippi. It is a very creative and lively place, hosting blues festivals and lots of American football games!

My family is Jewish. When we celebrate *Chanukkah*, we invite friends over to trade gifts, play *dreidel*, and eat lots of *gelt* (chocolate coins). On *Shabbat* (Jewish Sabbath), I always wear a white dress with my hair in a braid to temple. I'm not into makeup, or obsessing over my hair when it rains.

American football is my favourite sport. I love playing and watching it, even though boys say that girls can't play well. I'm determined to prove them wrong. I want to play in the NFL, and become a surgeon or a doctor working in the Emergency Room, too. That's my dream!

My cat Biscuit is the best in the world. My family says she's not because she sometimes bites and scratches, but she's very nice to me. I spend most of my day playing with her. My dog Rufus gets anxious and he always wants attention. My other dog, Bernie, is so funny. He makes this weird noise with his throat when he's excited. He has never growled, ever!

I got into the All State choir this year. We get to perform in New Orleans with different schools from around Louisiana. I love singing Taylor Swift songs with my friends.

Jewish sleep-away camp in Mississippi was so fun! I have a photo of my cabin up on my bedroom wall. I made so many happy memories and great friends that I organized a camp reunion once we were home.

I write letters when I'm passionate about causes. I wrote to Malala Yousafzai and she responded with a video! I also wrote to President Joe Biden about climate change. I'm proud of writing a letter to my principal asking for longer at recess. We got five extra minutes!

REBEL GIRL SUPERPOWER: **BEING BRAVE**

"Brave means not being afraid to try new things or be different."

Isabella

I want to be a good, kind person

Hawaiians are famously friendly people. The locals here will always treat you like family. No matter where you're from, everybody here is your cousin – we're one big *ohana*, which means "family" in Hawaiian dialect.

"Chào", "ciao", and "¡hola!" all mean "hello" – in Vietnamese, Italian, and Spanish (Chilean), which are my ethnicities. I learned Italian and Spanish at a young age and have worked hard to keep speaking them. I'm proud to have maintained my language skills.

I like to cook for myself. I take classes, and I make sure I practise what I've learned at home. My favourite thing to make is pasta because it's so versatile, but I have favourite foods from all my cultures: spring rolls from Vietnam, lasagne from Italy, and empanadas from Chile. Empanadas are traditionally stuffed with meat, half a hard-boiled egg, a black olive, and raisins, but I like mine with cheese.

I've been a Girl Scout since the age of five, and I plan on going until I'm 18. I have so many badges sewn to the back of my vest! I've always loved musical theatre, too. I've been in *The Little Mermaid, Newsies, Cinderella,* and *Robinson Crusoe*.

I'm passionate about human rights. I think it is important that people be treated the way they deserve, no matter their sexual orientation or colour of their skin. Homophobia and racism are just fancy words for hate, and hate is making the world unsafe and unkind. My dream job would be a detective because I find the study of criminology interesting, and I want to protect people.

Age: 13

My home:
I live with my mom, my dad, my grandmas, and my cheese-loving French bulldog, Amore. I have my own room. It has subtly colourful walls and my bookshelf is in rainbow order! I have lots of stuffed animals, a poster collage, LED lights, and a mirror that opens to reveal my jewellery hidden inside.

My town:
The state of Hawaii consists of 137 volcanic islands. I live on the island of O'ahu, in a small, beautiful beach town called Kailua. We have low buildings so as to protect the view of the Ko'olau Mountains. We can buy all sorts of food, but the local cuisine consists mainly of plate lunch, spam *musubi*, and poké bowls.

Madeline

Call me Maddy!

"I have no clue what I want to be when I'm older, I'm still a kid!"

Age: 10

My home:
I live with my mom, my dad, and my little brother, Jackson (8). I have my own bedroom with colourful flowers and birds on the walls; I love how they remind me of when I was younger.

My city:
Los Angeles (LA) is a huge city with sunny beaches, giant movie studios, and cool skyscrapers. People from all over the world come here to chase their dreams of becoming famous. You can spot movie stars on the streets and even visit the famous Hollywood sign!

I live a few miles from the ocean. It's usually sunny here and the water is always dark blue. It is busy and I often run into my friends. I joined the swim team this year at school. I'd like to be a lifeguard one day.

I usually eat cereal for breakfast. Lunch is peanut butter and jelly sandwiches with carrots, a cheese stick, and animal crackers, and for dinner I eat mac 'n' cheese or pizza. I love pizza – it's available almost everywhere and each person can choose the toppings they like.

Our school day always starts with morning exercises and walking the track before we head to the classroom. After school, I go to a recreational programme with my friends. I really like my aftercare teachers. They inspire me to be kind, never let anyone push me around, and to give others a chance even when they aren't doing the right thing.

I've been keeping a diary since second grade. I read a book called *Dork Diaries* that said writing in one can be soothing, and there were cool journals to buy at my school book fair so I decided to try it out. I write about my problems or how my day went. I recently went to a science camp with my fifth-grade class and wrote a lot while I was there. It makes me feel good to process my thoughts.

I'm part of America's Battle of the Books. It is a reading programme where we read novels from a list and compete against other schools on questions about them. I love that it introduces me to books I wouldn't have chosen myself! When I'm not busy reading I have started pet sitting. I have seven clients, with dogs, cats, chickens, a guinea pig, poisonous fish, and even a bearded dragon!

REBEL GiRL SUPERPOWER
I CAN MAKE ANYTHING OUT OF RECYCLED MATERiALS!

"I love that being creative with recycled materials can help the planet too!"

Rachael

I love trying new things

Age: 10

My home:
I live with my mom and my older sister, Olivia. My dad is remarried and lives in Michigan. My room is pink, just like my favourite dessert – cotton candy! It's cosy and makes me feel happy when I walk in. My favourite thing in it is my dolls' house. I made it myself, and I'm always creating new miniature pieces to decorate it with. It's my own tiny world where I get to be the designer.

My city:
I live in Eagle River, Alaska. It's a small town outside of Anchorage, where I go to school. I love being able to get bubble tea in the big city, but come home to nature. We are close to the mountains, trails, and parks. We have moose that sometimes walk down our street, and you can see the Northern Lights on really clear nights! My family likes to go hiking and sledding. The mountains here are huge and beautiful. They make me feel really small in a good way, like I'm part of something big and amazing.

We celebrate summer solstice in Alaska, when it's light outside for almost 20 hours! There's always a big street festival downtown. We stay out really late but it still looks like daytime. In winter, our days are super short. It's always dark when my mom drops me off at school, and when she picks me up. But it makes the snow sparkle, and that's kind of magical.

Mom says my hobby is "try-a-new" because I always want to try new things. I just learned how to knit and crochet. It's super fun even though I still drop stitches! My friends and I go skiing and ice-skating in the winter, and we like to swim indoors. We also spend a lot of time practising cartwheels, making friendship bracelets, or painting rocks. I like to organize when I'm alone, especially folding laundry.

I love turning trash into treasure. Sitting around a table with my friends, surrounded by glue, paper, cereal boxes, buttons, and string makes me so happy. We laugh, share ideas, and make a big mess. It's the best kind of fun! Give me cardboard, paint, and a glue gun, and I'll transform it into something awesome, like jewellery, games, doll furniture, or even a kaleidoscope.

My father is from Nigeria so I love spicy *egusi* soup. It is made with ground melon seeds. We eat it with *fufu*, which is soft and kind of tastes like potato. Since we can't always get it here, we make our own by mixing baking mix and instant potatoes. It's fun to eat because you scoop up the soup with your hands using the *fufu*! Alaska is more famous for freshly caught salmon. We even have salmon festivals!

I love clothes, and I especially like the business look. Wearing my yellow plaid jacket with a matching skirt and a yellow tie makes me feel confident and fancy, like I'm going to a big meeting. For special occasions, I have a beautiful dress that puffs out when I sit; it makes me feel like a cupcake!

SOUTH AMERICA

Argentina

Stretching through the tail of South America is Argentina. It is divided into distinct regions, each with its own climate. To the west, there are the snowy Andes Mountains. To the east lie thousands of kilometres of coastline hugging the Atlantic Ocean. The Pampas region is a grassland that appears to be totally flat for as far as the eye can see. To the north, there's tropical rainforest with gushing waterfalls. As the country extends down towards the South Pole, there are dramatic fjords and glaciers in the Patagonia region.

Wildlife Wonders

With so many climates, there are lots of different habitats for animals. As well as penguins, Patagonia is a haven for seals and sea lions who love the chilly conditions. The shoreline on the Atlantic Ocean is teeming with marine life, such as sharks, orcas, and dolphins. Elsewhere, there are magnificent jaguars, macaws, flamingos, and caiman.

Let's Dance

The tango is a dance that is thought to have originated in Argentina and neighbouring country, Uruguay. It spread across the world in the 20th century, and now has many different variations and styles. The dance is typically lively, high-energy, and passionate. A pair of partners glide across the floor hand-in-hand. The dance has lots of walking steps, too, so that performers can carefully consider their next move.

Goal!

Football is considered to be Argentina's most popular sport, with the men's national team claiming the World Cup three times. But another important pastime is *pato*. Teams compete for possession of a ball with the aim of throwing it in a net to score – while on horseback! *Pato* became the national sport of Argentina in 1953.

FAST FACTS

Official Name: Argentine Republic

Capital: Buenos Aires

Location: South America

Official Language: Spanish

Border Countries: Bolivia, Brazil, Chile, Paraguay, Uruguay

Currency: Argentine Peso

Population: 45.7 million

Area: 2,780,400 km²

Cowboy Culture

Gauchos are skilled animal handlers who, beginning in the 17th century, rode on horseback, herding wild horses, cattle and other animals across the Pampas grasslands. Traditionally they were dressed in ponchos, pleated trousers, and leather boots. They lived on the plains in huts made from mud and grass. In the past, it was considered a job only for men, but now, there are young women in Argentina training to be gauchos.

IGUAZÚ FALLS

Iguazú Falls

On the border of Argentina and Brazil are the Iguazú Falls, the largest system of waterfalls in the world. Two tiers of around 275 waterfalls curve around in a horseshoe shape. It is an incredible place of beauty, surrounded by a tropical rainforest. The sun frequently hits the water spray as it falls, creating rainbows.

Majestic Patagonia

The region of Patagonia, to the south of the country, is massive. Half of it is in Argentina, and the other half is just over the border in Chile. Though most of the area is covered in shrubland, there are dramatic views for hikers. The southern portion of the Andes extends here, and there are also towering volcanoes and a myriad of glacial lakes. Perfect for an adventure!

Did you know? Patagonia is home to the world's largest colony of Magellanic penguins. It's one of the largest penguin colonies outside of Antarctica.

REBEL GiRLS OF ARGENTiNA

Para-athlete **Lucia Montenegro** (b. 2001) won silver in the 100-metre wheelchair race at the Tokyo 2020 Paralympics, making her the 11th fastest junior women's wheelchair racer in the world.

Mercedes Sosa (b. 1935) from Tucumán, Tucumán Province, Argentina, was a folk singer and composer. She wrote a song for the Academy-Award-nominated film, *The Two Popes* (2019).

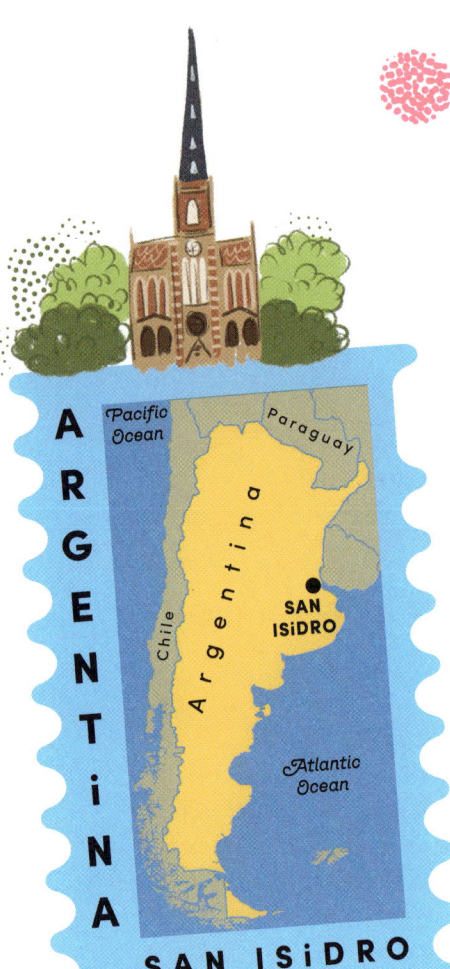

Ema

I want to be a choreographer

I take classical dance and jazz classes twice a week. This year, I'm starting at a secondary school specializing in the arts, where I will study Argentine folkloric dance and stage dance, too. I want to be a choreographer when I'm older; I love making up my own routines and watching gymnastics and synchronized swimming for ideas!

I have been going to Girl Guides since I was five. I would have started earlier if I could! I love working to earn the badges that I attach to my poncho.

I'm proud to be Argentinian, and I love learning about the history and culture of my country. I'm interested in the study of people and cultures in general – that's why I'd love to be an anthropologist if I'm not a choreographer when I'm older.

> "School can be fun, boring, interesting, and intense all at once!"

Pachamama Day is a thousand-year-old Inca tradition of honouring the Earth, and showing gratitude for its gifts. People hold ceremonies on 1 August, making offerings of food, and even burying small gifts in the ground to show respect and thanks for our food, water, and beautiful landscapes. It is a reminder to everyone to take care of the environment and appreciate the natural world around us!

I love my pets. We have a black dog called Chino, who is very active, a beige cat called Amelie, who sleeps a lot, and a calico cat called Lana, who likes to go out.

Romance and fantasy are my favourite book genres. My favourite books are *I Can Learn to Love You* by Agustina Cámara and *Insolent Women of History* by Felipe Pigna. Both are by Argentinian authors who I love.

Age: 12

My home:
I live with my mother, my father, my grandmother, and my two sisters, Violeta (19) and Malena (22). We speak Castilian Spanish at home. I have my own bedroom. In it, I have a wardrobe, a very messy desk, a bed, and a giant teddy bear!

My city:
I live in San Isidro, which is around 30 kilometres north of the city of Buenos Aires. San Isidro is one of the oldest cities in my region, with a beautiful cobbled centre, a neo-gothic cathedral, and beautiful riverside parks. The city is known as the national capital of rugby – we even have a rugby museum!

Brazil

Brazil covers half of the entire continent of South America. It shares land borders with every one of South America's countries, except for Chile and Ecuador. Around 60 per cent of the Amazon rainforest can be found here, and the mighty Amazon River dominates the north of the country. Each year, in February, you'll find revellers of from all over the world dancing to samba music at the biggest street party on Earth – the Rio Carnival!

FAST FACTS

Official Name: Federative Republic of Brazil

Capital: Brasília

Location: South America

Border Countries: Argentina, Bolivia, Colombia, French Guiana, Guyana, Paraguay, Peru, Suriname, Uruguay, Venzuela

Official Language: Portuguese

Currency: Real

Population: 212 million

Area: 8.515 million km²

City Living

Brazil's cities are bustling with energy. São Paulo is the biggest, whose skyline is dotted with skyscrapers, shopping malls, and apartment buildings. Rio de Janeiro is famous for its beautiful beaches, like Copacabana, where the locals meet to play volleyball as the sun sets. The Christ the Redeemer statue watches over the city. Brasília, the capital, was planned in the shape of an aeroplane. The government buildings are in the "cockpit", whereas the residential areas are in the "wings".

Rainforest Wildlife

Thanks to the Amazon Rainforest, Brazil is home to the most diverse animal life of any country in the world, including the greatest variety of monkey species anywhere on the planet. It's a place where electric blue morpho butterflies flutter past maned sloths, giant anacondas swim upriver, and jaguars stalk their prey.

Did you know? Around two million people attend Rio's Carnival each day.

Carnival Capers

During the five days leading up to the beginning of the Christian period of Lent, the streets of Rio de Janeiro transform into one giant party. People wearing incredible, colourful costumes dance at balls and in parades – sometimes through the night and well into the next morning! Samba schools compete for the awards for the best floats and costumes of the carnival before the important period of fasting and reflection of Lent begins.

Amazon River

The second longest river in the world, the Amazon flows through the Amazon rainforest, providing a lifeline for its plant and animal life, and a transport and trade link for the 1.5–2 million Indigenous peoples who live in small communities along its banks. Watch out for the world-famous omnivorous piranhas, who swim in the cool water. "Piranha" translates to "tooth fish" in the Brazilian language, Tupi. Piranhas replace their teeth throughout their lives, losing and regrowing them, just like sharks.

COPACABANA BEACH

Languages and Ethnicities

While most Brazilians speak Portuguese, 200 languages are spoken in Brazil. Most of these are Indigenous. That number was closer to 1,300 before Portuguese colonizers arrived in the 16th century, bringing their language with them. Today's Brazilian people descend from many different ethnic groups, such as the original Indigenous peoples and the Portuguese colonizers. Ancestors also include African people who were enslaved by human traffickers to work on plantations, which happened here in greater numbers than anywhere else in the world.

REBEL GiRLS OF BRAZiL

Regarded by many as the greatest woman footballer of all time, **Marta Vieira da Silva** (b. 1986), known as Marta in Brazil, has been named FIFA World Player of the Year six times.

Sonia Guimarães (b. 1957) was the first Black Brazilian woman to earn a PhD in physics. She is now a Professor of Physics at the Instituto Tecnológico de Aeronáutica.

Amora

My name means blackberry!

SÃO PAULO | BRAZIL

Age: 8

My home:
I live with my parents and my dog, Kika. I'm an only child. We mostly speak Portuguese at home, but sometimes I speak English with my dad. My room is very colourful. I decorate it with lots of stickers! I love letting Kika sleep in my room with me. She's my favourite!

Our surroundings:
I live in São José do Rio Preto in the state of São Paulo, which is the city I was born in. I still spend a lot of time there. It's a huge city. I love it because my cousin still lives there, so do the rest of my family, and a lot of friends! I love the museums and attractions; my favourite is the aquarium because there are lots of animals there, it's almost like a zoo.

Our national dish, *Feijoada*, is delicious! It is a stew made with black beans and pork. It's usually served with rice. For breakfast, I usually eat cheese on toast, or a fruit smoothie. I tend to eat out for lunch with my parents. We eat Brazilian food, like meat with rice or bread, and sometimes fries. I often eat vegetable soup for dinner, or pasta. And I love chocolate and grape ice cream!

I love celebrating Carnival. It's always such a huge party. I dance, eat traditional food, and dress up in the costumes my mother makes for me. She has a successful clothes store; I would like to work in fashion like her one day. I admire her very much. I really enjoy dancing, it's one of my favourite classes at school. We get to take circus skills lessons, too!

It's almost always sunny in Brazil. We are lucky to be able to play outside most of the time. I love going to play at the park with my friends. We get lots of breaks to play in the playground at school. I don't really play any sports, but I love watching football on TV, and I'd like to try tennis.

My puppy, Kika, is only seven months old. I love her so much! My parents gave her to me after I begged and begged. I help to take care of her, and she makes me very happy. I'm happiest when I'm eating sweets and cuddling her. The whole family loves her.

I love the Brazilian painter Tarsila do Amaral. She was born in the state of São Paulo just like me, and became a very important modern artist in the 1920s. I love the arts in general, that's why I like to visit museums in São Paulo. I am taking art classes at the moment.

> "I like to think I am good humoured most of the time."

Dance to the Beat!

Listen out in Colombia and you may hear the beats of salsa, cumbia, or reggaeton being played loudly at celebrations and festivals. One of the most famous is The Barranquilla Carnival, a four-day event that is one of the world's biggest carnivals. It blends Indigenous, African, and European traditions through music, dance, and parades.

Colombia

Known as the "gateway to South America", Colombia is right at the top of the continent, where it meets Central America. It is the only country in South America to have coast on both the Caribbean Sea and the Pacific Ocean. Colombia still feels the effects of Spanish colonization, and of the decades of civil war that followed independence, due to colonial legacies, but economic growth is one of the highest in Latin America. This forward-looking country is committed to developing renewable energy, so the future is bright.

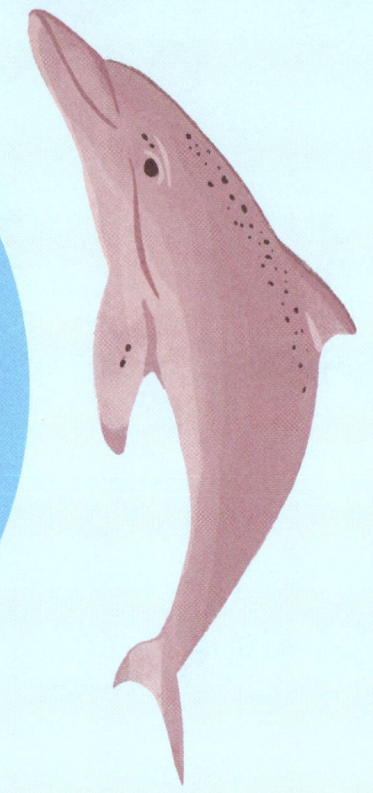

Nature's Rainbow

Home to more than 51,000 plant and animal species, Colombia is recognized as one of the 17 "megadiverse" countries on Earth. No wonder it produces marvels like the Caño Cristales River, called "the river of five colours", which turns into an aquatic rainbow at certain times of the year. Its bright colours might look like magic, but are caused by a weed a bit like algae or moss, called *Macarenia clavigera*. The pink river dolphin can also be found in many of Colombia's rivers.

FAST FACTS

Official Name: Republic of Colombia

Capital: Bogotá

Location: South America

Border Countries: Brazil, Ecuador, Panama, Peru, Venezuela

Official Language: Spanish

Currency: Colombian Peso

Population: 52.89 million

Area: 1.14 million km²

CAÑO CRISTALES RIVER

Pedal Power!
Colombia is the cycling capital of Latin America. Its mountainous terrain is the perfect training ground for keen riders. Colombian cyclist Egan Bernal won the Tour de France in 2019, making Colombia proud on the world stage, and inspiring a new generation of fans.

Food of Colombia
The *Bandeja Paisa* (Paisa platter) is Colombia's most famous dish. It is full of variety and is brought out to celebrate special occasions. It is served on a huge plate – or platter – and usually consists of white rice, *arepa* (filled flatbread), chorizo (or sausage), fried plantain, *chicharrón* (fried pork belly or rind), avocado, black or red beans, minced beef, and a fried egg. Yum!

Little Candles Day
Most people in Colombia observe the Catholic faith. On Día de las Velitas (Little Candles Day), Catholics light candles and paper lanterns, placing them all over their towns, cities, and villages to celebrate the Virgin Mary. Pavements, balconies, and windowsills are covered in seas of twinkling light. When you light a candle it is customary to pray for someone, and to give thanks.

Did you know? Colombian children often enjoy coffee with milk (café con leche) from a young age.

Precious Emeralds
Colombia is one of only a few places on earth where emeralds form in shale rock instead of igneous rock. The geological processes lead to less iron being present in these emeralds, which means stones of a more intense green. Greener emeralds have higher value to potential buyers. The emerald industry contributes significantly to Colombia's economy and creates jobs, but it doesn't always meet human rights and environmental standards – issues that organizations in Columbia are working hard to fix.

REBEL GIRLS OF COLOMBIA
Suffragist **Esmeralda Arboleda Cadavid** (b. 1921), fought for women to have the vote. Her work helped bring in a new law in 1954 that allowed women to vote. She went on to become Colombia's very first woman senator.

Athlete, politician, and former weightlifter **María Isabel Urrutia Ocoró** (b. 1965) from Colombia won the first ever gold medal for Colombia at the Summer Olympic Games.

Salomé
My family calls me Salito

Dad takes me to school on his motorbike every day. Wearing our uniform is compulsory. School is really fun, our teachers take us to the park during breaks and I learn something different in every lesson. We learn in English as well as Spanish. Sometimes we go on school trips by coach.

Dressing up at Halloween is so much fun. I go out trick-or-treating at night with my family. We usually end the evening with a delicious frisbee dinner outside – where your meal is served on the underside of a frisbee, like a plate. You can play a game of frisbee with it afterwards!

Sancocho de pollo is a hearty Colombian soup. It is a traditional dish that we make with chicken, potatoes, yuca, corn, and plantain. I love it! I also enjoy *ajiaco* (which is a different type of spicy soup), pasta, sausages with potatoes, meat with guacamole, hamburgers, tamales, ice cream, fruit, and rice pudding.

I love to draw anime and watch anime series. I collect anime cards, too! I'm passionate about the art of drawing and aspire to be a truly great draftswoman one day. My mom is so supportive; it makes me happy when my mom or my teacher appreciate the drawings I give them. If I don't end up drawing professionally I would like to be a vet or an actor.

We have a cat named Chimuelo (meaning toothless!), who is very naughty, playful, and spoiled. We also have two goldfish. One is called Rosa and the other is named Shinobu, after one of my favourite anime characters.

Age: 9

My home:
I live with my mom and dad and I have my own room. It is decorated with coloured lights and anime posters, and I stick my drawings on the window. I have lots of stuffed toys, anime figurines, and comics.

My city:
I live in Bogotá, the capital of Colombia. It's one of the largest and most populous cities in the world. It is high up in the Andes mountains where it is cool much of the time. Some people call it "The Fridge of Colombia"! It has an historic, cobbled centre, as well as more modern buildings sprawling out to the outskirts. We have plenty of parks, shops, museums, restaurants, and multiple amusement parks!

REBEL GIRL SUPERPOWER: BEING SOCIABLE. SOMETIMES I TALK A LOT!

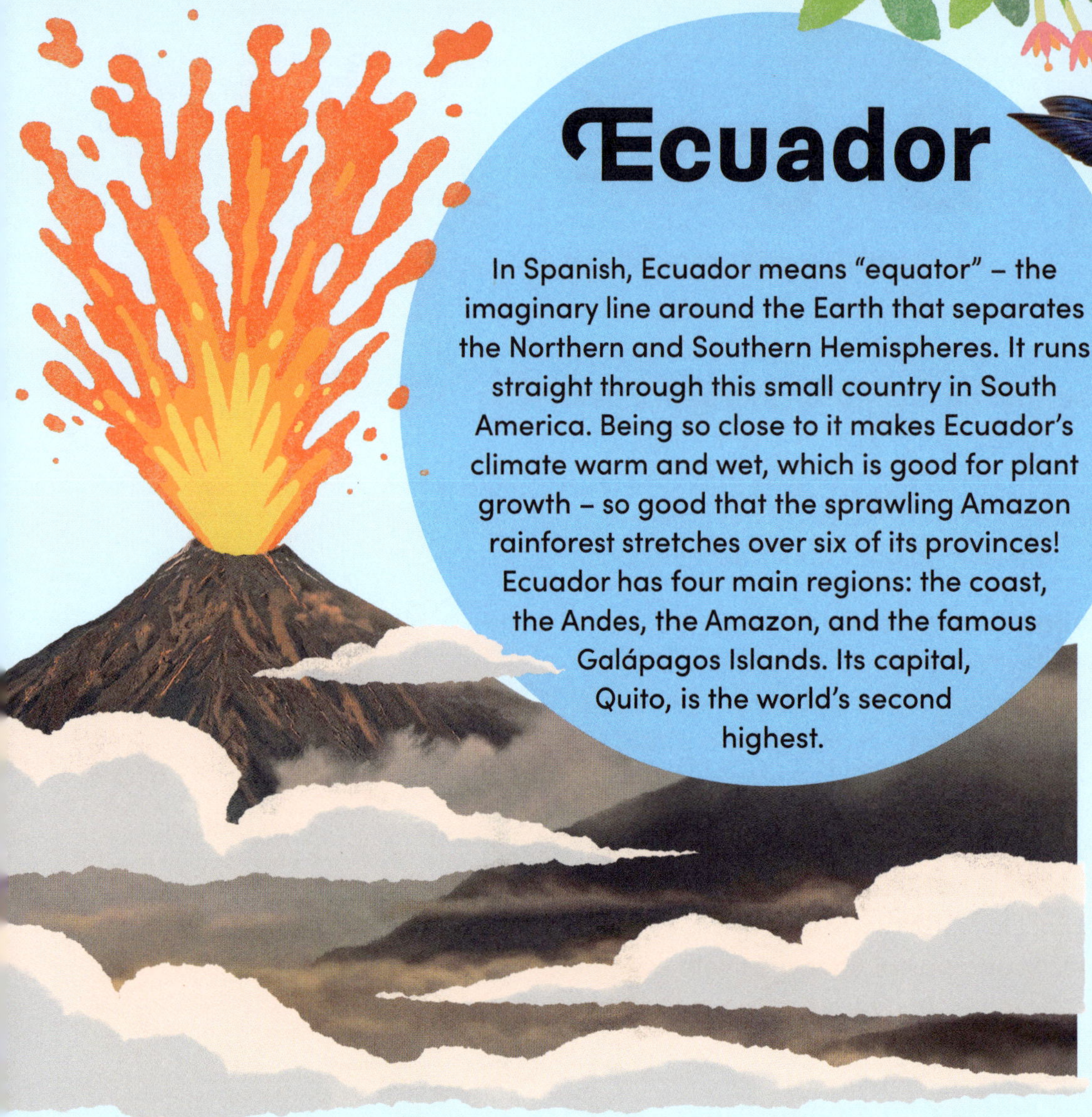

Ecuador

In Spanish, Ecuador means "equator" – the imaginary line around the Earth that separates the Northern and Southern Hemispheres. It runs straight through this small country in South America. Being so close to it makes Ecuador's climate warm and wet, which is good for plant growth – so good that the sprawling Amazon rainforest stretches over six of its provinces! Ecuador has four main regions: the coast, the Andes, the Amazon, and the famous Galápagos Islands. Its capital, Quito, is the world's second highest.

Avenue of the Volcanoes

The Andes mountain range may offer incredible views, but watch out! A large number of its peaks in Ecuador are active volcanoes. Most are located in a 400-kilometre stretch known as "The Avenue of the Volcanoes". Each one is distinctive, inspiring local folklore giving them individual personalities. Cotopaxi is the world's highest active volcano at 5,897 metres, Mama Tungurahua (known locally as "Throat of Fire") has erupted four times since 1999, and Quilotoa is home to a beautiful emerald-green crater lake.

Amazing Amazon

This truly immense rainforest is the world's largest. It is ten times the size of France! More plant and animal species live here than anywhere else on Earth: sloths, capybaras, hummingbirds, macaws, toucans, purple passion flowers, and orchids are just some of them. In 2008, Ecuador became the first country in the world to grant constitutional rights to nature. This means that here, nature legally has the right to exist without human interference.

FAST FACTS

Official Name: Republic of Ecuador

Capital: Quito

Location: South America

Border Countries: Colombia, Peru

Official Language: Spanish

Currency: US Dollar

Population: 18.1 million

Area: 283,560 km²

The Quechua Community

The Quechua people make up the largest Indigenous community in Ecuador, with many distinct regional groups. Northern Quechua is the second most spoken language in the country, after Spanish, which was imposed by Spanish colonists in the 16th century. Quechua culture has a rich woven textile tradition, and each region has its own unique patterns, using symbols like the sun, rivers and stars.

All Aboard!

A *chiva* (also Spanish for goat) is a special type of bus used across Ecuador and other parts of South America. They are hand painted, usually in the bright yellow, blue, and red colours of Ecuador's flag. Most have a ladder to the rack on the roof, which is used for carrying people and livestock in rural communities. In cities like Ecuador's hilly capital, Quito, some of them have been converted into mobile party buses. Locals rent one for special occasions and drive around town in them, dancing and listening to music.

QUILOTOA CRATER LAKE

Grub's Up

Each region of Ecuador has its own distinct foodie specialities. On the coast, seafood and coconut flavours are common: a favourite dish is *ceviche*, a tasty seafood salad. In the mountains, people eat a lot of potatoes, corn, and meat, including roasted or fried *cuy* (guinea pig), which is eaten on special occasions. Ecuador is one of the world's biggest exporters of bananas.

Did you know? The Galápagos tortoise can live to be more than 100 years old!

The Galápagos Islands

Made up of 19 islands and more than 100 islets in the Pacific Ocean, the Galápagos Islands are famously where Charles Darwin studied the incredible wildlife that helped him to form his theory of evolution. Unique creatures like giant tortoises and blue-footed booby birds live here and nowhere else on Earth! It is a world-leading destination for eco-tourism, teaching visitors how to respect and protect the environment.

REBEL GiRLS OF ECUADOR

Sumak Helena Sirén Gualinga (b. 2002) is a "Climate Hero" from the Kichwa Sarayaku community in Pastaza, Ecuador. She fights for the rights of people in the Amazon, and for environmental protection.

Nemonte Nenquimo (b. 1985) formed an Indigenous environmental campaign that resulted in a 2019 court ruling protecting 500,000 acres of Amazonian rainforest and Waorani territory from oil extraction.

Nicole

Singing makes me feel like me

Age: 11

My home:
I live with my mom, my dad, my brother, Manuel (7), my godfather, and our two Shetland sheepdogs. I have my own room. It's basic but comfy. One of the walls has a tree covered in beautiful pink butterflies on it. I love my comfy bed most!

My city:
I live in a suburb called Cumbayá in our capital city, Quito. The city has colourful old buildings, big churches, and a lot of parks. We are high up in the Andes. It's not too hot or too cold here since we're close to the equator – so close that we can drive right to it! You can even stand with one foot in each hemisphere.

I mostly eat home-cooked Peruvian food, because that's where my parents are from. My favourite dish is called *llapingacho*: a tortilla made mostly out of potatoes. You fry it and it is the perfect balance between crunchy and soft. I like it best with a little bit of chili.

Our country is experiencing almost daily blackouts. Drought throughout Ecuador has put our national power grid under so much strain recently that the electricity shuts off. Sometimes the power is out all day.

My family has a tradition of spending Christmas in Peru, when it's summer there, not winter! I love the fact that we can go to the beach and feel hot in the day, and enjoy a more cosy feeling at night when it's cool.

"The emotion you put into a song can make it something unforgettable to listen to."

We only have five minutes to run between classes at school. If you are late you get a tardy pass! Some classes I love, like music and drama, but some I don't enjoy so much, like maths and science. It's funny, I seem to get better grades in the classes I don't enjoy. The teachers think I talk too much!

The hobbies I love most are acting, dancing, and singing. When I sing, I try to let all my negative thoughts out, and have a moment to be who I really am. I'm not a great singer yet, but practice always helps. I'm excited to have a small role in my school play. We rehearse every day.

I have recently joined a new friendship group. My new friends make me feel more confident about myself and have made me much happier. We talk and laugh together, and we do things no one else understands, like just throwing ourselves on the floor laughing. None of us understand why we find it so funny, but we do.

Peru

Once the heart of the Inca Empire, Peru is home to the breathtaking ruins of Machu Picchu, an ancient city nestled amongst the clouds in the eastern Andes. The Andes run down Peru like a spine, separating the dry plains on the west coast from the hot, wet Amazon rainforest in the east, which covers half of the country. Most Peruvians live in cities like the capital, Lima, but some communities in the Altiplano plateau farm on steep mountain sides, using methods passed down for generations.

Incan Legacy

The Incas ruled from the 15th to the 16th century, building a vast empire in the Andes known for its advanced farming techniques, architecture, and roads. While their ruling class was of the Quechua ethnic group, the empire included many different peoples. In the 1500s, Spanish colonists displaced many people across the region, but Indigenous traditions and languages, like Quechua, thrive in today's Peru. Sixty per cent of Peruvians have an Indigenous ancestor, descending from peoples such as the Aymara, Achuar, and Shipibo.

The Spectacled Bear

The only species of bear in South America, the spectacled bear, can be found in the high forests of northern Peru. Nature lovers can take a trip to see the animals that inspired one of the most beloved fictional bears in the world: Paddington! Spectacled bears don't really eat marmalade. Instead, they feast on fruit, cacti, and the soft parts of palm trees.

In Peru llamas are often adorned with bright tassels and textiles, to signify ownership and showcase their cultural importance.

Woolly Helpers

Peruvians have been farming terraced slopes in the Andes for more than 10,000 years. They grow more than 3,500 types of potato there. But they wouldn't be able to do it without a host of woolly helpers: llamas, alpacas, vicuñas, and guanacos (all related to camels) are perfectly suited to the high pasture. They provide meat and milk, their dung is used as fertilizer, they carry heavy loads up the steep slopes, and their wool is used to create socks, hats, and ponchos. No wonder they are highly valued in Peruvian culture. The Incas even carved llama statues out of gold.

FAST FACTS

Official Name: Republic of Peru

Capital: Lima

Location: South America

Border Countries: Bolivia, Brazil, Colombia, Chile, Ecuador

Official Languages: Spanish, Aymara, Quechua

Currency: Peruvian Sol

Population: 34.2 million

Area: 1.285 million km²

Machu Picchu

Known by some as the "Lost City of the Incas", Machu Picchu is the ruins of a 15th-century city and a UNESCO World Heritage Site. People travel from all over to trek the the Inca Trail through the incredible Andes mountains, emerging at the old city's walls. Built without mortar, with bricks that fit together tightly, it was an incredible feat of engineering. It lay hidden beneath overgrown forest until 1902, when Agustín Lizárraga Ruiz, a Peruvian farm worker, stumbled upon it while looking for new land for crops.

UROS ISLAND | LAKE TITICACA

Did you know?
There are more than 70 species of frog in Peru, many are brightly coloured to warn predators that they are poisonous.

Queen of the Andes

Peru may be famous for the incredible vegetation of the Amazon rainforest, but have you heard of the "Queen of the Andes"? This majestic plant grows on rocky slopes and can reach 15 metres tall. It grows for up to 100 years before blooming! After blooming, it produces thousands of seeds then dies.

REBEL GIRLS OF PERU

Susana Esther Baca de la Colina (b. 1944) is a reknowned Peruvian singer–songwriter, school teacher, folklorist, and three-time Latin Grammy Award winner. She studies the evolution of music.

Renata Flores Rivera (b. 2001) is a Peruvian Quechua singer and rapper. Her music empowers Indigenous youth and promotes the Quechua language on a global stage.

Lake Titicaca

The largest lake in South America, Lake Titicaca, sits 3,812 metres above sea level and is shared with Bolivia. The Inca people believed it was the birthplace of the sun. The lake is most famous for its human-made islands, constructed from totora reeds. They provide floating homes for the Uros people.

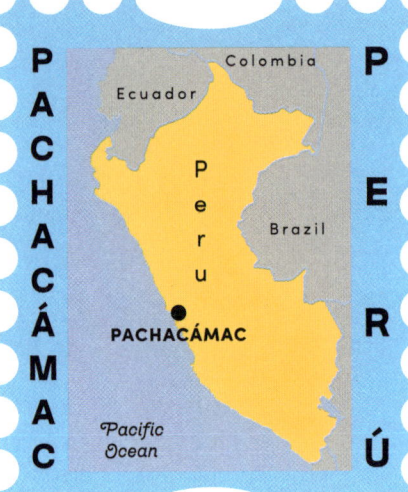

Camila

I'm a big thinker

Age: 9

My home:
I live with my parents and my two brothers, Vasco (6) and Salvador (4). We speak both English and Spanish at home. I have my own room and I have LEGO® sets, books, markers, and notebooks everywhere. I always write down ideas and things that interest me. What I like most about my room is the beautiful view. It's a space where I can imagine, create, and learn in peace.

My village:
Pachacámac is a quiet place surrounded by nature. We are 40 kilometres southeast of Lima, in the valley of the Lurín River. It is very green. We also have the huge archaeological zone of Pachacámac, a very important site in the history of Peru. It houses lots of temple ruins – some of the most amazing artefacts have been found there. It was first settled around 200 CE.

The Temple of the Sun at Pachacámac was built by the Incas. It was built for the Sun God, Inti. The Inti Raymi (Festival of the Sun) is still an important ceremony in Peru. At the Sacsayhuamán archaeological site near Cusco, it is celebrated each year with a huge re-enactment of ancient Inca rituals. There are costumes and dances, and Andean music is played on instruments like panpipes and drums.

"Causa" is Peruvian slang for "friend", "buddy", or "dude". But it is also the name of a typical Peruvian dish! *Causa* is made of layers of mashed potato filled with chicken, tuna, or anything you like, really. It is served cold. We also eat a lot of stews, vegetables, and meat. *Ceviche* is the most famous dish in Peru, it is raw fish marinated in lemon with onion and chili.

I always go to the library during recess. I am an avid reader, and love to devour books on all sorts of topics that allow me to discover new worlds and ideas. My favourite are *The Little Prince* by Antoine de Saint-Exupéry, *Sapiens* by Yuval Noah Harari, and *The Toothpaste Millionaire* by Jean Merrill, in which Rufus and Kate start their own toothpaste company in the sixth grade. I dream about being the CEO of my own company one day, too!

I have lots of hobbies, including music, dance, theatre, and art. My favourite sports are football, volleyball, swimming, and cycling. I love spending time with friends. We play outside, or we have fun painting and watching movies together.

I love to research space. I have just learned about stellar nucleosynthesis. It's the process by which stars create heavier elements from lighter ones, leading to the formation of important elements like carbon, oxygen, and iron, which are the essential building blocks for life.

MARSHALL
ISLANDS

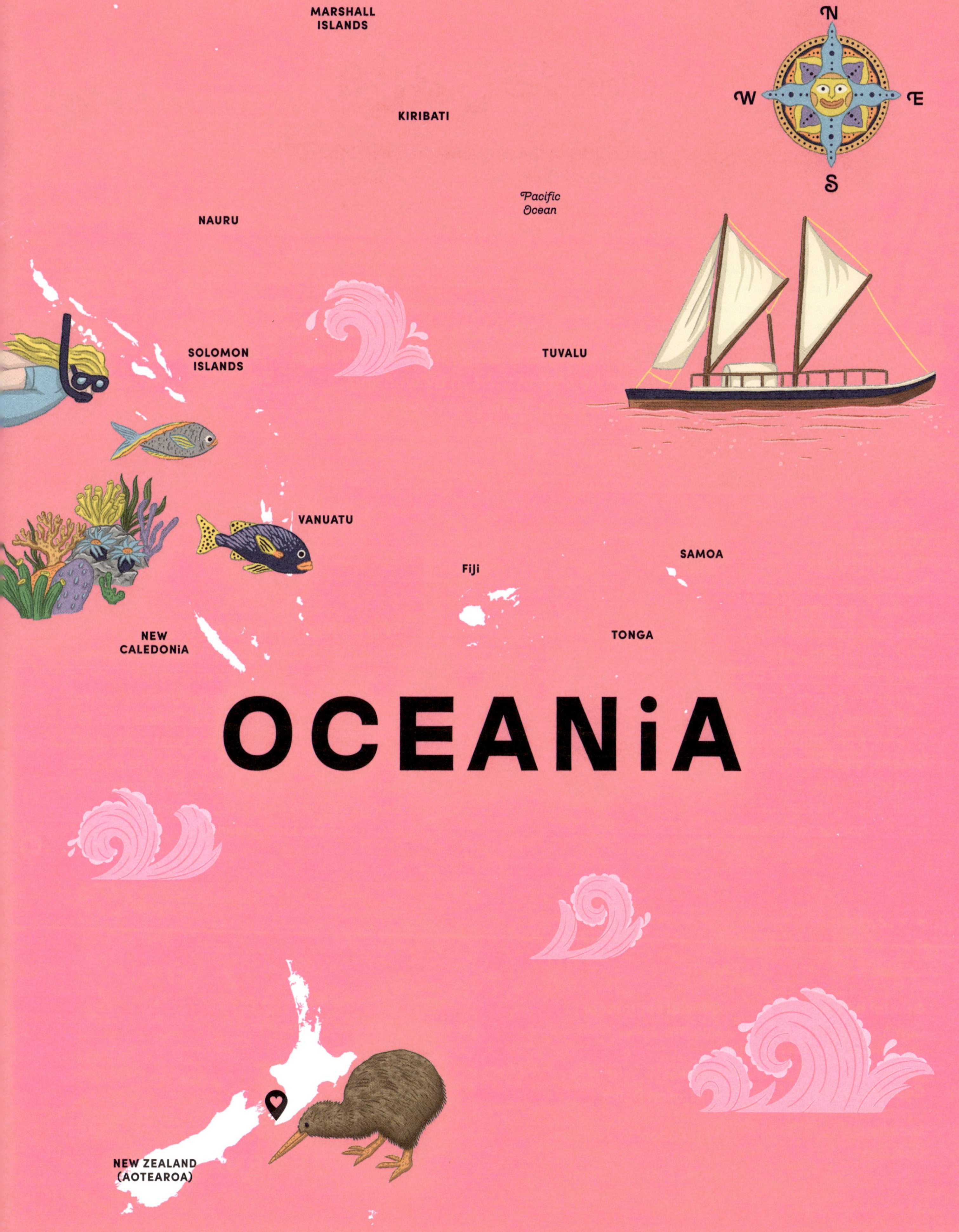

KIRIBATI

NAURU

Pacific
Ocean

SOLOMON
ISLANDS

TUVALU

VANUATU

SAMOA

FiJi

TONGA

NEW
CALEDONiA

OCEANiA

NEW ZEALAND
(AOTEAROA)

Australia

This country – the only one on earth that is also a continent – is far into the Southern Hemisphere, where it is summer from December to February. It is the smallest of the seven continents, and also one of the world's largest islands – it's about two-thirds the size of all of Europe combined. It is famous for its warm, sunny climate with more than 3,000 hours of sunshine a year, and Australians are taught from a young age to be safe in the sun by wearing sunscreen, hats, and sunglasses.

Did you know? It does snow in Australia! You can ski and snowboard in the mountains of southern New South Wales and northern Victoria.

Outback Adventures

The Outback is the name for the huge inland area that covers around 70 per cent of Australia, yet is home to less than five per cent of the population. The environment is very diverse, from rainforests to deserts, and it's thrumming with lots of different wildlife. Dingoes, emus, and kangaroos roam free.

First Nations People

Aboriginal and Torres Strait Islander peoples have lived in Australia for over 65,000 years. The Anangu peoples consider Uluru in central Australia a deeply sacred site. Rising from the surrounding plains, Uluru is a vast geological formation known as an inselberg. The Anangu peoples believe it was created by ancestral beings and are dedicated to protecting both Uluru and the land around it.

FAST FACTS

Official Name: Commonwealth of Australia

Capital: Canberra

Location: Oceania

Official Language: English

Currency: Australian Dollar

Population: 27.2 million

Area: 7.741 million km²

ULURU

Sporting Nation
In 2025, 61 per cent of Australian adults who exercised chose to do so outside. Whether it's Aussie rules football, cricket, lawn bowls, or tennis, there's always sport to be enjoyed.

Aussie Animals
Australia's incredible animals are world famous, from cute-looking kangaroos, koalas, and possums, to deadly crocodiles and snakes. Around 80 per cent of the wildlife is endemic to Australia, meaning it can only be found here. The platypus is a unique egg-laying mammal with the bill of a duck and a beaver-like tail. It even produces pink milk!

Ocean Beauty
The Great Barrier Reef, off the coast of Queensland in northeastern Australia, is the world's largest coral reef system and living structure. It is home to thousands of species of marine life, and is so big it can even be seen from space!

Colonial Past
Britain first sent colonists to Australia in the 18th century. These were mainly convicts, to solve the British problem of overcrowded prisons, but also free settlers. The impact of colonization on First Nations people and their lands was violent and long-lasting. The colonial period ended in 1901, and today, work is ongoing to right the wrongs done to the First Nations people during this era.

SYDNEY OPERA HOUSE

REBEL GIRLS OF AUSTRALIA
Dr Romaine Moreton (b. 1969) is a writer and also the CEO of a First Nations owned and led media research production company that centres the stories and languages of Aboriginal Peoples.

Author and illustrator of *The Illustrated Encyclopaedia* series and the *How We Came To Be* series, **Sami Bayly**, (b. 1996) is a natural history illustrator who champions ugly and unusual animals.

Willow

I enjoy making costumes

I eat a mixture of Australian and Turkish food. My mum is Turkish Cypriot and my dad is Australian. My favourite meal is a Turkish breakfast with eggs, olives, halloumi, cucumber, fresh Turkish bread, and hot aniseed tea, which I help my mum prepare. My favourite Australian food is a meat pie smothered in tomato sauce – yum!

We visit nearby Rottnest Island every year. It can only be reached by ferry, and you have to ride bikes to get around. We love cycling to the beach and enjoying big barbecues with friends. My favourite bit is feeding the cute little furry quokkas, which are native to the island.

I do ballet, jazz, and tap lessons. I've been going since I was three, and the end-of-year concert is always a highlight. My favourite so far is *The Nutcracker*. I love learning new routines and making up my own choreography at home in my mum's dressing-room mirror.

I play in a netball team, and have been to watch a couple of West Coast Fever matches. Meeting the professional netball players afterwards was so inspiring.

I love to be creative. I have made some special fancy dress costumes out of colourful supplies from my craft desk. Mary Poppins and a 100-year-old lady were such fun outfits to design. I won best costume during Book Week at school for the giant rabbit riding a London bus that I made from the book *Ruby Red Shoes Goes to London*. This year I dressed up as Matilda; I even carried a drinking glass with a floating newt in it as a prop!

Age: 9

My family:
I live with my mum, dad, and my brother, Dylan (6), who I share a bunk bed with. Our room is decorated in a woodland theme with a feature wall in pine-tree wallpaper. We have lots of animal toys.

My city:
I live in a small suburb of Perth called Bassendean. It feels like a big country town with a tight-knit community, yet we are only 15 minutes from the centre of Perth. Perth is very hot, very sunny, and is the largest city in Western Australia.

"I really enjoy being creative with my routines and costumes."

Clementine

... but everybody calls me Lemon!

Age: 11

My home:
I live in a white house with my mum, dad, brother, Henry (15), and sister, Bertie (7). My bedroom is upstairs. We have a veranda and a garden with a kennel in it, where our two dogs, Banjo and Lola, sleep. They are big German Shorthaired Pointers. It's my job to walk them every night!

My city:
Newcastle is the second biggest city in New South Wales on the east coast of Australia. We have many beaches, two ocean baths, beautiful nature reserves, and a huge salt-water lake. Newcastle was built on the land of the Awabakal and Worimi peoples.

¶ I'm happiest with my friends – surfing, paddle boarding, or just swimming at the ocean baths near my house. We sometimes see whales and dolphins! On dry land, we chat, do crafts, make jewellery, play on the computer, and have sleepovers. Sometimes we create our own musicals!

¶ I like to eat pavlova, a traditional Australian dessert made with meringue, whipped cream, and fruit. My grandma always makes it for me for my birthday. She's there for me through thick and thin.

¶ We have a caravan, and my family drives to remote beaches or the Outback for holidays. We take bikes and find trails to ride on. I love waking up in nature. We eat sunrise brekkies on our fold-out picnic table, listening to the galahs, cockatoos, and lorikeets singing to each other.

¶ I'm excited to be Sports Captain this year at school. I love netball, touch rugby, and surf lifesaving, and I play Aussie rules football in an all-girls team. We train after school and play matches at the weekend. I cheer so loudly when I go to support my team, the Sydney Swans. The only problem is my dad and grandad support our rivals, the Hawks!

¶ I enjoy horse riding at my grandparents' farm, where we muster cattle. I sometimes go to pony camp during the school holidays. It's a long drive away so I stay there for a week. We sleep in dorms, get our horses ready in the morning, and do lots of riding practice. It's hard work, but I love it.

¶ My neighbour Jean is 101 years old. I visit her a few times a week. She lives on her own and has carers who deliver her food and help her in the evenings. I love talking to her about her memories.

REBEL GIRL SUPERPOWER: MY CARING NATURE

"I love being active outdoors and being social. Paying sport lets me do both at once!"

North to South

The North Island is the most populated of the two main landmasses, despite being smaller. Around 76 per cent of citizens live here, mostly in urban areas, including Wellington, the capital, and Auckland, the largest city. To the south, there are some amazing sights, such as Milford Sound/Piopiotahi, an enormous fjord; Abel Tasman National Park, which is a tropical coastal paradise; and the snow-peaked Franz Josef Glacier/Kā Roimata o Hine Hukatere.

New Zealand

In the Tasman Sea, to the southeast of Australia, is the island country of New Zealand. It is split into two main landmasses, the North and South Islands, that are connected by a short ferry ride. More than 600 smaller islands also make up the nation of New Zealand, or Aotearoa as it is known in the Māori language. New Zealand sits on the Pacific "Ring of Fire", a semi-circle-shaped region in the Pacific Ocean prone to volcanic activity and earthquakes. Up to 200 mostly minor quakes are felt each year.

Did you know?
In 1893 New Zealand became the first country to allow women to vote.

FAST FACTS

Capital: Wellington

Location: Oceania

Official Language: English, te reo Māori, New Zealand Sign Language

Currency: New Zealand Dollar

Population: 5.3 million

Area: 268,838 km²

Island Wildlife

New Zealand's remote location means that its animals have evolved in unique ways. It has many flightless birds, such as the kiwi, the takahē, and the kākāpō – sometimes known as the owl-faced parrot. This is also a wonderful place to spot marine creatures. You can watch whales on the waves, including orcas, humpbacks, and sperm whales.

Lights, Camera, Action!

New Zealand's incredibe landscapes have been used as a backdrop for numerous films and TV shows. Towering waterfalls, rugged mountains, and lush forests are perfect for bringing dramatic stories to life. One of the most famous is *The Lord of the Rings* series. Some of the sets built for filming, such as the fictional village of Hobbiton, can still be visited today.

FRANZ JOSEF GLACiER/ KĀ ROiMATA O HiNE HUKATERE

Māori Revival

The Māori have lived in New Zealand for over a thousand years, but in the 19th century, British colonizers came, violently seizing land, and suppressing Māori culture and language. Major protests in the 1970s led to an ongoing tribunal that has awarded reparations and led to laws changing. In recent times, there has been a surge in Māori people studying their pre-colonial language, te reo Māori, and reviving cultural traditions such as the art of *moko*, a sacred tattoo that is a symbol of heritage and tells stories within its designs.

The All Blacks

Rugby is New Zealand's favourite sport. The national women's squad is called the Black Ferns and the men's squad is the All Blacks. Before a match, both teams perfom a ceremonial Māori dance called the *haka*. The *haka* has thousands of variations, and the Black Ferns perform the *Ko Ūhia Mai*, while the All Blacks perform the *Ka Mate*. These *haka* inspire the players to come together in unity and strength, ready to overcome the challenge ahead.

REBEL GiRLS OF NEW ZEALAND

Jacinda Ardern (b. 1980) is a New Zealand politician who in August 2017 became leader of the New Zealand Labour Party. From 2017–2023, Jacinda served as the country's prime minister.

Lisa Carrington (b. 1989) is a canoeist of Māori and European descent. She's New Zealand's most successful Olympian thanks to her five gold medals from the 2012, 2016, and 2020 Olympic Games.

Molly

I love to read and dance!

Age: 10

My home:
I live with my mum, my dad, my brother, Teddy (8), and our little sister, Hazel (4). I have my own room. I have a bed, a desk, and a beanbag. I have lots of posters on my walls, and fairy lights. All my books are on shelves. My favourite thing in my room is definitely my bed!

My city:
Eastbourne is a small village in Wellington Harbour. We can get to Wellington city by ferry, or by car. There is one main primary school. We have a small row of shops, a few playgrounds and parks, and lots of beaches to swim at. In summer, we like to jump off the wharf and swim to the raft.

We speak English and te reo Māori at school. We don't have to wear a uniform. Our main subjects are reading, writing, maths, PE, art, and structured literacy. We also do *Kapa haka* every Wednesday morning, when we practise traditional Māori action songs and chants.

Matariki is a special time in New Zealand; it is Māori New Year when a special cluster of stars appears, in either June or July. We sing traditional *waiata* (Māori songs) about the stars. There are nine stars and *Matariki* is the mother star. We cook a big meal to symbolize the different stars and enjoy spending time with family (*whānau*).

I dance twice a week with a hip-hop dance crew. It's a big commitment and we train hard. We are a mix of ages and I love my dancing friends. I'm proud when we are performing together. I am also learning Highland dancing. My great-grandmother, Molly, who I am named after, was born in Scotland. It's nice to feel connected to her.

I'm happiest when I'm camping at the beach. We go to the same camping ground with my cousins every year in the summer. We live in different parts of New Zealand so it's very special to be together, swimming in the sea and rivers, going for bush walks, riding bikes, and eating ice cream!

I'm passionate about reading and writing. We have an amazing librarian at school and I am training to be able to help her at lunchtime. I like to read series like *Harry Potter*, and I also loved *Percy Jackson and the Keeper of the Lost Cities*. I like fantasy books the most, but I also enjoy school stories about kids the same age as me.

When People Move

Did you know? 43 million people are refugees globally.

People move for all sorts of reasons: for work, to keep themselves or their family safe, or just through choice, to experience a new way of life. Moving can be difficult. It might involve learning a new language, starting a new school, trying new foods, making new friends, or leaving the things you love behind. It can also offer new perspectives, broader opportunities, and a fresh start. Let's explore what it's like to start a new life in a different city, country, or continent.

USEFUL DEFINITIONS

Migrant
A person who moves to a new place for any reason, either by choice or to find safety.

Immigrant
Someone who moves to a new country with the intention of staying there to build a new life.

Refugee
A person who is unsafe in their country due to war, persecution, or violence and is forced to flee. Refugee status gives them protection under international law.

Asylum Seeker
Someone who has applied for refugee status, but is waiting to receive a decision. Seeking asylum is a human right.

Moving for Work
Some people's jobs involve relocating temporarily and bringing their family with them. They might work for their government, in the military, or for a charity. Other people move permanently for better opportunities. They might be looking for higher wages, better working conditions, or a chance to learn new skills. Many countries have programmes to match workers from other places with jobs, helping both the workers and the economy of the country they move to.

Moving by Choice
Some people move to be nearer to family, others simply decide they can live a better quality of life somewhere else, even if it is far away from the life that they know. Maybe they want to experience a different culture, climate, or education system. Or maybe the access to medicine and healthcare is better where they are going. Things that make people want to leave their homes are called "push" factors; "pull" factors are things that make people want to move.

Moving for Safety
Some people need to escape dangerous situations, such as war, domestic violence, or famine. Refugees flee their countries because of threats to their lives, personal freedom, or human rights. They may be at risk because of war, or be facing persecution based on their nationality, race, religion, social group, or political opinions. Many countries have laws to protect people who arrive looking for safety, offering them a chance to rebuild their lives.

New Flavours

The movement of people is reflected in food all over the world. Patagonia has its Welsh community to thank for the *bara brith* tea bread available in towns across the province of Chubut. In Germany, kebab is the most popular street food since the migration of Turkish workers in the 1960s. More recently, US chefs invented the sushi burrito, which fuses Japanese, Mexican, and American cuisines.

Sushi Burrito, San Francisco

Chicago River, St Patrick's Day

Chinatown
NEW YORK

Berlin Turkish Kebab

Bara Brith, Wales

Blending Cultures

People bring their language, art, and music with them when they move, enriching their new homes. The Greek Quarter in Melbourne, Australia features striking Hellenistic architecture in celebration of its large Greek community, and Chinatowns are another example of visually distinct neighbourhoods that appear all over the world as a legacy of Chinese migration. The Chicago River is dyed green every year on St Patrick's Day, to celebrate the contributions of Chicago's Irish immigrants.

What Can You Do?

Being kind to new people can make a big difference. If you notice a new student looking lost at school, help them find their way. Once you have got to know them, you may learn about their culture. Tell them what you love about yours too.

REBEL GiRL MiGRANTS

Yusra Mardini (b. 1998) is a swimmer and a refugee of the Syrian civil war, having fled in 2015 by boat. A year later, she represented the first Refugee Team at the Summer Olympics in Rio (2016). She is dedicated to advancing access to sports and education in refugee communities.

Actress, businesswoman, and entrepreneur **Jessica Alba** (b. 1981) grew up on different Air Force bases across the United States. Reflecting on that time, she says, "I was really sad to leave [...] – it's such a safe environment, and everyone on base becomes your family."

Gauri

My nickname is Kachoo

Age: 11

My home:
I live with my father, mother, and grandmother. My bedroom is very simple. I have a few posters with positive and funny slogans on the wall. My favourite says, "Sorry, I have *plants* this weekend". My bedroom is always covered in books that I'm half-way through reading. My room makes me happy.

Where we live:
We live in an apartment in the Tarapore Officers Enclave in Delhi. It's a colony for people serving in the Indian Armed Forces and their families. My father is in the Indian Navy so we move around. There are lots of apartment buildings here. The area is quiet, but it gets noisy in the evening when kids come out to play and people are returning from work. We have two huge parks. There is a replica Army tank in the main field. All the kids try to climb it!

We move whenever my father is transferred. His Navy job takes him all over India. We have lived in Visakhapatnam, Mumbai, Karwar, Delhi, Mumbai again, Delhi again... and we will be here until he is stationed elsewhere! My father is often away on official work. I remember visiting him when he was sailing once, when I was little. At the time he was only able to come back during festivals.

I travel to school in an Army school bus. In every naval station we have lived in, we have had access to an Officers' Institute (OI). It is a nice place to meet friends, have dinner, or play badminton. My father takes me swimming there in summer. We sometimes attend fun OI events for military families, like Diwali Night or Christmas Carnival.

"I love the Hindi word for firefly, 'jugnu'. They spread a tiny bit of light wherever they go."

Clubs helped me to make friends here. When we got to this colony, I enrolled in football classes. Then, when I became interested in Western dance, my mother signed me up for that, too. I have friends whose fathers are in the Army and Air Force as well as the Navy. I love walking in the colony with them, chatting.

Navaratri is a festival in honor of Durga, a Hindu goddess. *Kanya puja* is performed on the eighth day of nine when girls are worshipped as we are said to embody Durga. I invite my friends, and my mum and grandmother place red *dupattas* on our heads and offer us food. They touch our feet, and give us gifts. It makes me feel very special.

I love reading about history, especially the Tudors. My dream job is to become an author so I can write fantasy novels inspired by Tudor history! I'm in Theatre Club at school. We practise street plays and learn to make theatre masks. I'm also teaching myself the ukulele using YouTube tutorials.

Jo

Having a sister really helps

Age: 10

Where we're from:
Gatineau is a small city in Québec, Canada, on the Ottawa River. Both French and English are spoken there. It has a lot of green spaces and you can skate on the Rideau Canal when it freezes over each winter. Our mom is a diplomat, so we moved to Cambodia a year ago for her work. We will be in Cambodia for two years before moving back to Canada.

REBEL GIRL SUPERPOWER: MY ENTHUSIASM FOR LIFE!

My teacher introduced me to a big friend group when we moved. They are really nice, and over the year that I have been in Cambodia I have made more friends, all from very different backgrounds. They speak lots of different languages because we go to an international school. We really like learning about their different cultures.

If I didn't have my sister, moving would have been much harder. We have been able to talk to each other when it has felt difficult. Bringing our dog, Rebel, from home has been comforting, too. She is a labrador mix who loves swimming and licking our faces. She is a very playful doggy. Snuggling with my dog and eating ice cream are my two favourite things!

In Canada we used to share a room, but in Cambodia I have my own! I love having a place to keep my things. I like to knit and crochet little bunnies. I have improved at it so I give them to people as gifts.

Most Khmer food has meat in it and I am vegetarian, but I do like curry. I don't eat meat because animals are my friends. I miss Canadian poutine. Yum!

Elsa

We've had new adventures

Age: 13

Where we live now:
Phnom Penh is a very big city with a lot of modern skyscrapers and some very old temples. Cambodia is a mainly Buddhist country and people greet each other with a kind of bow called *sampeah*, not a handshake. We've seen lots of interesting celebrations in the streets here: funerals, religious ceremonies, and monks saying prayers.

REBEL GIRL SUPERPOWER
THAT I'M FASCINATED BY THE WORLD

Moving here was a culture shock! We had never lived anywhere other than our house in Canada, we had no idea what to expect. When we first got here everything was so different. Everyone spoke a different language and there were tons of things to learn. We have travelled so much more in the time since we left than in the rest of my life combined!

It took a little while to make friends, because we arrived halfway through the year, but I have a really good group now; some are from different grades who I met through activities. In Canada, we hung out at each other's houses or outside. Here, we hang out at school or sometimes at the mall.

I'd love to be an aerospace engineer at NASA (or the Canadian space agency!) when I'm older. I recently won second place in the Cambodian round of the World Mathematics Championships. My other passion is baking. I'd love to have my own bakery. I read a lot, I play piano, football, and volleyball, and I am in the cross-country running club.

We travel in three-wheeled vehicles called tuk-tuks here. They are open-air and have a bench in the back without any seatbelts! In Canada we mostly drove our family car.

Eleanor

Missing home is hard

Age: 11

Where I'm from:
I was born and raised in Melbourne, Australia. I miss the outdoor food markets, taking trams everywhere, walking in the city gardens, swimming at the city pool, and all the animals. Every afternoon, lorikeets, by the thousands, filled the trees by my apartment. They squawked until the sun dipped below the skyscrapers. I miss their comforting noise.

Where I live now:
My mum and I moved to Minneapolis, USA. Now we live in a townhouse in a quiet area. When we moved, I got to choose the paint colour for my walls. It's called "swimming" (a sea green). I also picked out a colour for my sheets, called "pool" (an aquamarine). So my room is a "swimming pool", which makes me feel calm and happy. My grandparents live in Minneapolis but the rest of my family is still in Australia.

Moving continents wasn't easy. Mum and I had to leave for our safety, so we came quickly with four suitcases. I shipped some of my books, toys, and games, but it took more than a year for everything to arrive. We had a very empty house at first. My cat, Señor Nevado, had to stay in Melbourne. I miss him very much. My mum and I have been through a lot. We love each other even when we're mad or upset about life.

In Australia I would always wear a wide-brimmed hat, and my favourite sports were rock climbing and surfing. Here, I dress for warmth, and I play in the snow! I've tried sledding, snowboarding, snowshoeing, snow tubing, skiing, and ice-skating. I love to swim. The rhythm of doing laps back and forth soothes my busy mind.

I really love science. I like to make up experiments in my kitchen with my chemistry set. Sometimes I get a little carried away mixing spices from the pantry! I'd love to be a vet when I'm older. I volunteer a few times a month at the local animal shelter, reading to the animals and taking them for walks. I understand how hard it must be for them to wait for their forever family. I try to help them feel comforted and loved.

People have sometimes made fun of my accent here. When I have found it hard to feel part of the community in my new country, I have always been able to escape into books. It comforts me to know that the characters have gone through similar challenges that I have.

I loved the Melbourne International Film Festival. Mum and I would watch the Spanish language kids' movies, and go out for big bowls of ramen after. Sitting on milk crates, we'd slurp the broth and laugh. I attend a Spanish Immersion school in Minneapolis. The teachers are really nice; many are from different countries, like me.

Francesca

I've lived all over the world

We have lived on three continents so far! My dad is a US diplomat so we move every three years. His previous posts were in Brazil and Angola. Occasionally, I get to talk to friends from Angola online. I love being able to stay connected with them. I try to call my very best friend every other Friday. She still lives in Angola. I see her as my sister. I have regular video calls with my grandparents in the USA and Colombia, too.

Mom is Colombian and Dad is from California, so I'm Colombian American. I have always talked with both of my parents in their native languages. We still use a few words of Portuguese from when we lived in Brazil and Angola. I speak English at school. Since most of the kids are Dominicans, sometimes we communicate with each other in Spanish.

My friends are from the embassy compound as well as school. We do lots of things together! We build forts, play video games, watch movies, and have pillow fights. We talk about school, play with our pets, make up games, and go to the pool. I have basketball practice with my school friends twice a week. On Tuesdays, I'm on the swim team with my friends from the embassy. Every night, I rollerblade around the compound with them while my mom walks our dog.

I want to be a children's or YA author and a lawyer. I love animals, so would love to work with them, but not as a vet because I have trypanophobia (fear of needles), and will almost faint if I see anybody getting an injection or blood test! I'm excited to be doing a Junior Vet Camp this summer.

I love everything about soccer! Except for playing it. I support Liverpool and my brother is an Everton fan. They are rival teams, which makes it fun. My baseball team is the LA Dodgers because I'm a California Girl!

Age: 10

My home:
I live with my mom, my dad, my brother, Joseph (13), and our dog, Cappuccino, who came with us from Angola. We live on a US embassy compound. I have my own room. The walls are painted lavender and white. My bed has a blanket with a map of the USA on it. I have a window seat, where I read and write. I made posters of my favourite sports teams as extra decoration.

My current city:
I live in Santo Domingo, the capital of the Caribbean island nation of the Dominican Republic. Spanish is the main language here, and it's hot year-round. Unfortunately, there is a lot of traffic. I have to leave for school really early. Sometimes there are hurricanes, but none of them have seriously affected the city while I've lived here. People like to dance merengue, Son, and bachata, and they play music very loud! Baseball is huge in the DR, too.

How We Made This Book

Studio shoot of Aiva holding a basketball, which was later replaced by an illustration of the world

Finding, getting to know, photographing, and drawing more than 70 girls (and their pets!) from around the world took a lot of work from a passionate global team of editors, designers, picture researchers, cartographers, photographers, and illustrators. Let's take a look behind the scenes at how we made this book.

Yifan's Chinese dragon – from sketch to colour

How were the girls chosen? We put out a casting call across all continents looking for Rebel Girls aged 8–13 around the world to tell us about their lives and who inspires them. We picked girls from as many different countries as possible whose answers richly described life there. We chose multiple girls in some countries where there is a large population or where we were able to show how people live in different areas. We always tried to showcase different personalities, interests, and experiences!

What challenges were there? In some countries the internet was unstable, which made contacting the girls' families difficult. Some girls live in remote areas; finding a photographer who could get there was tough. Some girls were shortlisted for the book but couldn't be featured in the end, for reasons of access, cultural sensitivity (being photographed wasn't supported in their culture), or for safety (their location needed to remain confidential). We thank them for taking the time to fill in the application.

What about language? Many of our girls answered the questionnaire in English, even if it wasn't their first language. Some answered in their native language and the editorial team translated them. We learned a lot of new words!

How about the facts? This book is packed with facts! All of the information, pictures, illustrations, and maps in the book have been vetted by a fact-checker, a geography consultant, a cartography team, a picture research team, and a cultural sensitivity reader.

How did the photoshoots work? Some girls were photographed at home using a portable backdrop and lights. Some were invited to a photographer's studio. We tried to make photoshoots fun, playing the girls' favourite music and providing snacks! Most girls wore three or four different outfits and we chose the photo that best represented them at the end.

How did we choose the outfits? We didn't! The girls got to choose "something that represents YOU!", sometimes based on a selection of hobbies or interests that we wanted to showcase in the book. Some girls brought props relating to their hobbies, some even brought their dogs! All wore their own clothes.

Helpful Organizations

Room to Read is a global education organization that develops children's foundational literacy skills, as well as life skills that promote gender equality. Girls supported by their programming in Bangladesh, Cambodia, Laos, Nepal, Sri Lanka, and Tanzania completed interviews and attended photoshoots. **The World Association of Girl Guides and Girl Scouts** passed on our casting call to girls in areas we would otherwise have missed. We thank these organizations for the work they do in empowering girls and young women around the world.

Millie and her pet dog Arlo behind the lens

Sidney making fun shapes

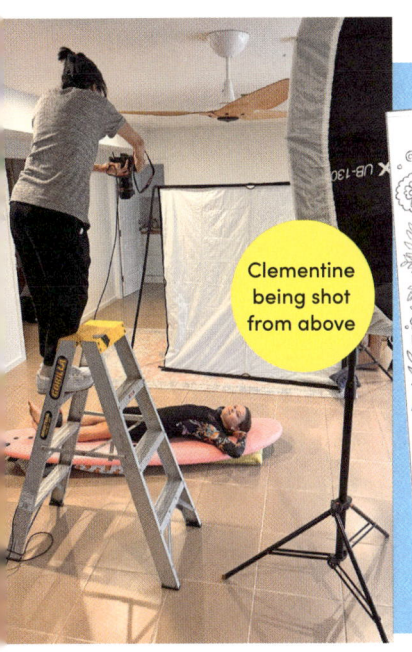

Clementine being shot from above

Frieda's sketch for Beatriz

Ana's sketch for Arya

Tinuke's sketch for Nathalie

Not all pets were cooperative!

Willow posing as Matilda at home

Sinem hand cutting paper for Anna, Avalon, and Willow

About Rebel Girls

Rebel Girls, a certified B Corporation, is a global, multi-platform empowerment brand dedicated to helping raise the most inspired and confident generation of girls. The brand purposefully creates content, products, and experiences to empower Generation Alpha girls and equip them with the knowledge and tools they need to thrive. Because confident girls will radically transform the world.

Good Night Stories for Rebel Girls

Let the stories of real-life women and girls entertain and inspire you. Each volume in the Good Night Stories series includes 100 tales of extraordinary women.

Check out these mini books too! Each one contains 25 tales of talented women, along with engaging activities.

Growing Up Powerful

Filled with helpful advice, Q&As between experts and girls around the world, and fun quizzes, the Growing Up Powerful series has the inside scoop on all things girlhood and helps tweens and teens become their most confident selves.

Cook with some of the most famous women chefs working today! And enjoy 100+ mouthwatering, kid-tested recipes.

Dig deeper into the lives of five real-life heroines with the Rebel Girls chapter book series.

Go on more incredible middle-grade adventures with **Secret Society of Rebel Girls**.

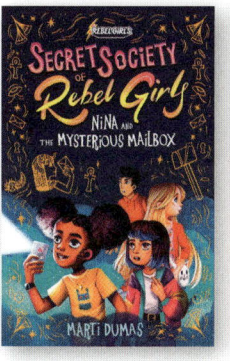
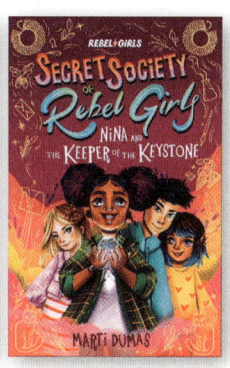

Enjoy interactive books and gift sets!

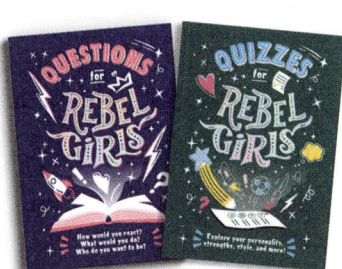
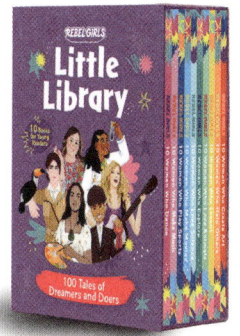
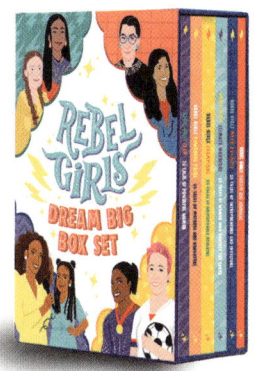

ViSiT REBELGiRLS.COM

Learn more about the Rebel Girls universe and find tons of confidence-boosting content at **rebelgirls.com**. Listen to hundreds of exciting audio stories on **Rebel Girls' award-winning app and anywhere you listen to podcasts.** Check out Rebel Girls clothing, jewelry, toys, puzzles, and more. And get the inside scoop on all things Rebel!

WATCH ON YOUTUBE!

Step into the Rebel Girls universe on YouTube and discover a world of inspiring stories, fun animations, and empowering adventures made for girls, by girls. Watch exclusive episodes, behind-the-scenes content, and interviews with changemakers from around the globe.

Join the Rebel Girls community on YouTube. Scan the QR code or visit **youtube.com/RebelGirls** to start watching!

Credits

The publisher would like to thank the following for their kind permission to reproduce their photographs:

(Key: a-above; b-below/bottom; c-centre; f-far; l-left; r-right; t-top)

4 Katja Hentschel: (br). **Ko Sasaki:** (bl). **Amit Machamasi:** (tr). **Kerttu Malinen:** (crb). **Manuel Soares:** (tl). **5 Tabitha Arthur:** (cr). **Joseph Fox:** (tl). **Tatiana Fernández Geara:** (br). **Emma-lee Hacker:** (clb). **Alejandra San Miguel:** (tr). **9 El-bachir Rhazaf aka Bachir Photo:** (tc/Morocco). **Régis Binard:** (tc). **Chris Chen:** (tl). **Liesa Cole:** (c). **Dasha (Lapina Darya):** (bl). **Jeremy Meek:** (crb). **Roar Paaske:** (br). **Emily Quinn:** (cl). **Saiyadeth:** (tr). **Kristen Thompson:** (cr). **12 Dreamstime.com:** Gabriel Araujo (crb); Fabian Plock (tr). **Getty Images:** AFP / Gianluigi Guercia / Staff (cl). **13 Dreamstime.com:** Vladislav Jirousek (bl). **Getty Images / iStock:** gabrielsarabando (tc). **Getty Images:** PICHA Stock (cr). **15 Manuel Soares. 16 Alamy Stock Photo:** Nature Picture Library / Ernie Janes (c). **17 Alamy Stock Photo:** Sorin Colac (bl). **Dreamstime.com:** Sean Pavone (crb); Rechitan Sorin (tr). **18 El-bachir Rhazaf aka Bachir Photo. 20 Dreamstime.com:** Kierran Allen (c). **21 Alamy Stock Photo:** David Salvatori / VWPics (tr). **Getty Images:** Molly Darlington - World Rugby (cla). **23 Oliver Kruger. 24 Dreamstime.com:** Znm (ca). **25 Dreamstime.com:** Hel080808 (cr); Janina Kubik (tr); Pakhnyushchyy (clb). **26 Jonathan Seni. 29 Jonathan Seni. 32 Getty Images:** Dan Kitwood (br). **Dreamstime.com:** Nilanjan Bhattacharya (cl); Md Shahanur Islam (tr). **33 Dreamstime.com:** ElloriaVoltan (cra); Kamrul Hasan (clb). **35 Monon Muntaka. 36 Monon Muntaka. 38 Dreamstime.com:** Petr Maek / Petrmasek (tl); Olena Serditova (c). **39 Dreamstime.com:** Michal Jurczyk (tl); Lach Sotheara (tr); Ke Nguyen (cb). **Getty Images:** Robertus Pudyanto (cl). **40 Régis Binard. 42 Régis Binard. 44 Alamy Stock Photo:** View Stock (c). **45 Alamy Stock Photo:** IanDagnall Computing (bl). **Dreamstime.com:** Chuyu (cra). **Fotolia:** Eric Isselee (cr). **47 Sean Gallagher. 48 Sabrina Miso. 51 Milos Gazdic. 52 JunXin Zeng. 54 Dreamstime.com:** Dvd Fotos (br). **Getty Images:** Debtanu Das (cl). **55 Alamy Stock Photo:** Stockbym (tr). **Dreamstime.com:** Liqiang Wang (clb). **57 Ritam Banerjee. 58 Reuben Singh. 60 Alamy Stock Photo:** mauritius images GmbH / Jose Fuste Raga (c). **Dreamstime.com:** Oleg Pidodnya (crb). **61 Alamy Stock Photo:** Patrick Batchelder (tl). **Getty Images / iStock:** Korkusung (clb). **63 Ko Sasaki. 64 Dreamstime.com:** Masar1920 (cl); Oskanov (br). **65 Dreamstime.com:** Boris Medvedev (tl); Turfantastik (bc). **66 Dasha (Lapina Darya). 68 Dreamstime.com:** Buntoon Rodseng (c). **69 Dreamstime.com:** Parawat Isarangura Na Ayudhaya (cr); Saylakham Khayongek (tl); Panom Bounak (tr); Nhut Le Quang (bl). **71 Saiyadeth. 72 Alamy Stock Photo:** Thomas Marent / Rolfnp (cra). **73 Dreamstime.com:** Matyas Rehak (crb); Ymgerman (cla). **75 Black Cat Studio. 76 Dreamstime.com:** Jianqing Gu (c). **77 Dreamstime.com:** Bdingman (tl); Jasper Neupane (cra); Jordan Tan (clb). **79 Amit Machamasi. 80 Amit Machamasi. 82 Alamy Stock Photo:** Noppasin Wongchum (c). **83 Alamy Stock Photo:** Sean Pavone (tr). **Dreamstime.com:** Sosharp (cl). **85 Samuel He. 86 Dreamstime.com:** Panya Khamtuy (cl); Sean Pavone (br). **87 Dreamstime.com:** Le Cong Duc Dao (clb); Byungsuk Ko (tl). **88 Alamy Stock Photo:** Nattee Chalermtiragool (bl). **89 Tim Franco "Propaganda Studio Limited". 90 Alamy Stock Photo:** Tuul and Bruno Morandi (crb). **Dreamstime.com:** Ulrich Allgaier (tl); Wzj0930 (c). **91 Alamy Stock Photo:** Jan Wlodarczyk (c). **Dreamstime.com:** Inuella365 (bl). **93 RTR - Subhash Semasinghe. 96 Dreamstime.com:** Biletskiy (cl); Copora (tr). **97 Dreamstime.com:** Sean Pavone (tl). **99 Roar Paaske. 100 123RF.com:** grigory_bruev (cl). **101 Dreamstime.com:** Ttretjak (tr). **101 Dreamstime.com:** Dmitry Chulov (clb). **Getty Images:** Silvia Otte (cr). **102 Kerttu Malinen. 104 Dreamstime.com:** Jenifoto406 (cl); Aleh Varanishcha (cr). **105 Dreamstime.com:** Bhofack2 (cl); Thecriss (tr); Valleysnow (cr); Iryna Kulinchyk (cb). **107 Magali Delporte. 108 Dreamstime.com:** Jenifoto406. **109 Alamy Stock Photo:** robertharding / Markus Lange (cl); **Getty Images:** Marco Prosch (cra). **110 Kalle Singer. 113 Katja Hentschel. 114 Dreamstime.com:** Maglara (c). **115 Dreamstime.com:** Carafoto (tl); Schnapps2012 (cr); Ivan Cernicky (clb). **116 Nikos Tsiros. 118 Dreamstime.com:** Boarding1now (br); ShutterUpIreland (clb). **118-119 Dreamstime.com:** Darkbird77 (t). **119 Alamy Stock Photo:** Peter Cavanagh (tr); Panoramic Images (cr). **120 Emily Quinn. 122 Alamy Stock Photo:** Calin Stan (c). **123 Alamy Stock Photo:** Jan Wlodarczyk (c). **Dreamstime.com:** Alberto Masnovo (bl). **Getty Images / iStock:** Zolga_F (cr). **125 Andrea Giacomelli. 126 Alamy Stock Photo:** Pictorial Press (tl). **Getty Images / iStock:** JacobH (b). **127 123RF.com:** Sborisov (cr). **Dreamstime.com:** Andrew Balcombe (tr). **128 Yvette Glasius. 131 Jeremy Meek. 132 Dreamstime.com:** Sean Pavone (c); Oleksandr Prykhodko (b). **133 Dreamstime.com:** Lukasz Janyst (tr); Natalia Mylova (cla). **135 Pau Storch. 136 Dreamstime.com:** Radu Cadar (cl). **137 Dreamstime.com:** Milan ierny (crb); Lukaszimilena (tr); Igor Kupčo (cl). **139 Zuzana Krajci. 140 Dreamstime.com:** Olga Itina (cl); Lunamarina (tr). **141 Alamy Stock Photo:** mauritius images GmbH / Jose Fuste Raga (r). **Dreamstime.com:** Tomas1111 (cl). **143 Joseph Fox. 144 William Anthony. 147 Mario De la Torre Rodriguez. 148 Dreamstime.com:** Alexander Shalamov (br). **Getty Images / iStock:** yes-thats-it (cl). **149 Dreamstime.com:** Ryhor Bruyeu (cr); Alexander Mychko (tr). **150 Daniel Holmgren. 152 123RF.com:** Eric Isselee / isselee (c). **Alamy Stock Photo:** Scott Wilson (br). **Dreamstime.com:** Sorin Colac (bl). **153 Dreamstime.com:** Olga Miltsova (tl); Michael Zech (b). **155 Oleksandra Kosenko. 156 Dreamstime.com:** Tawatchai Prakobkit (c). **157 Alamy Stock Photo:** David Pearson (cla). **Dreamstime.com:** EMFielding (cb); Luciano Mortula (bl). **159 Bradley Secker. 160 Dreamstime.com:** Pmstock (c). **161 Alamy Stock Photo:** Derek Croucher (tr). **Getty Images / iStock:** ivanastar (cla). **163 Greg Funnell. 164 Matt Thomas. 167 Jamie Lau. 168 Greg Funnell. 170-171 Matt Marcus. 173 Aled Llywelyn. 176 Alamy Stock Photo:** Ben Queenborough (cra); Robert McGouey / Wildlife (br). **Dreamstime.com:** Volodymyr Byrdyak (tl); Frank Fichtmueller (tr). **177 Dreamstime.com:** Ahkenahmed (clb); Robert Cocquyt (tr). **179 Emma-lee Hacker. 180 Richmond Lam. 182 Dreamstime.com:** Jedynakanna (cra); Galyna Andrushko (r). **183 Alamy Stock Photo:** Walter Bibikow / DanitaDelimont (bl). **Dreamstime.com:** Irishka777 (cla). **184 Logan C Thomas. 187 Amanda Baker. 188 Alamy Stock Photo:** Science History Images / Photo Researchers (ca); Bill Waterson (tl). **Getty Images / iStock:** RolfSt (br). **189 Alamy Stock Photo:** Michele Falzone (tl); Geopix (crb). **190 Laura Moss. 193 Anjali Pinto. 194 Liesa Cole. 197 James Peck. 198 Alison Bell. 201 Lara Everly (So She Did LLC). 202 Lena Lee. 206 Dreamstime.com:** Martin Schneiter (cl). **207 Alamy Stock Photo:** Michele Falzone (tr). **Dreamstime.com:** Cristian Martin (cla); Minnystock (bl). **209 Javier Pierini. 210 123RF.com:** marchello74 (r). **211 Alamy Stock Photo:** robertharding / Alex Robinson (tr). **Dreamstime.com:** Ekaterinabelova (cl). **213 Luis Souza. 214 Dreamstime.com:** Kobby Dagan (cl); Iralgo74 (br). **215 Dreamstime.com:** Luis Echeverri Urrea (tl). **216 Victoria Holguin. 218 Alamy Stock Photo:** Image Professionals GmbH / Per-Andre Hoffmann (cla); Mammals of Panama by Oyvind Martinsen (cra). **Dreamstime.com:** Ondrej Prosicky (tr). **219 Dreamstime.com:** Albertoloyo (tr); Pablo Hidalgo (cl); Richard Espenant (bl). **221 Daniel Maldonado. 222 Dorling Kindersley:** Gary Ombler / University of Pennsylvania Museum of Archaeology and Anthropology (ca). **Dreamstime.com:** Galyna Andrushko (r). **The Metropolitan Museum of Art:** The Michael C. Rockefeller Memorial Collection, Bequest of Nelson A. Rockefeller, 1979 (cla). **223 Alamy Stock Photo:** Ionut David (t). **Dreamstime.com:** Libux77 (cr). **225 Alejandra San Miguel. 228 Getty Images / iStock:** rudi_suardi (c). **Shutterstock.com:** Alexandre.ROSA (br). **229 Dreamstime.com:** Nico Smit / Ecophoto (crb); Vlad1949 (tl). **Getty Images / iStock:** africanpix (bl). **230 Frances Andrijich. 233 Chris Chen. 234 Dreamstime.com:** Natheepat Kiatpaphaphong (c). **235 Alamy Stock Photo:** Action Plus Sports Images (bl); Vincent Lowe (tr). **237 Tabitha Arthur. 239 Alamy Stock Photo:** Inge Johnsson (cr). **Dreamstime.com:** Vichaya Kiatyingangsulee (c); **Getty Images / iStock:** Kai_Wong (cb). **241 Reuben Singh. 242-243 Simon Toffanello. 245 Kristen Thompson. 246 Tatiana Fernández Geara. 250 Richmond Lam. 251 Frances Andrijich:** (bc). **Chris Chen:** (cl). **Greg Funnell:** (tr). **Sean Gallagher:** (bl). **Samuel He:** (c/Arya). **Jamie Lau:** (tl). **Anjali Pinto:** (c). **Pau Storch:** (cr)

Cover images: *Front:* **Magali Delporte:** c; **Milos Gazdic:** br; **Monon Muntaka:** tl; **James Peck:** tr; **Jonathan Seni:** bl; **Luis Souza:** bc; *Back:* **Frances Andrijich:** cr; **Amanda Baker:** cl; **Ritam Banerjee:** tl; **Black Cat Studio:** bl; **Greg Funnell:** br; **Richmond Lam:** tr; **Daniel Maldonado:** tc; **Anjali Pinto:** bc

Meet the Illustrators

Aurélia Durand is a French illustrator known for her vibrant, inclusive art. Her digital illustrations often feature diverse characters and celebrate Black culture, self-love, and joy.

Sinem Erkas is a British designer and artist with Turkish-Cypriot heritage. As well as illustrating some pages in this book (all hand cut out of paper) she art directed all of the other illustrators on their spreads.

Tinuke Fagborun is a British-Nigerian illustrator. Her vibrant, optimistic art celebrates diverse storytelling, and challenges dominant narratives surrounding women of colour, creating empowered and rich portrayals.

Caribay Marquina is a Venezuelan artist based in Argentina. Her vibrant illustrations blend fashion, nature, and a nostalgic longing for her homeland. She creates commercial and editorial work for global clients.

Frieda Ruh is a German illustrator and lettering artist. She adorned all the beautiful maps in this book. She loves working with bold colours in the hope that her bright designs make grey days more colourful.

Ana Strumpf is a Brazilian artist globally recognized for her colourful, pop, and playful style. Her "Re. Cover" project, illustrating on magazine covers, brought her international acclaim, building on her background in fashion and interior design.

Libby VanderPloeg is a California-based artist and illustrator. She is known for her whimsical, colourful maps, and her modern, light-hearted vignettes that celebrate community.

Yifan Wu is a Chinese artist based in the USA. Blending conceptual depths with visual allure, her work – spanning a wide range of styles – often uses visual analogies to convey complex ideas.

 Penguin Random House

Acquisitions Project Editor Sara Forster
Project Art Editor Stefan Georgiou, Cristina Antequera
Senior Production Editor Jennifer Murray
Senior Production Controller Mandy Innes
Senior Acquisitions Editor Katy Flint
Temporary Managing Editor Hazel Eriksson
Design Manager Vicky Short
Art Director Charlotte Coulais
Publishing Director Mark Searle

Art Directed and Designed by Sinem Erkas
Written and Edited by Sarah Harland with Emma Roberts
Picture Researchers Ceri James and Claire Guest
Illustrations by Aurélia Durand, Sinem Erkas, Tinuke Fagborun, Caribay Marquina, Frieda Ruh, Ana Strumpf, Libby VanderPloeg and Yifan Wu

Cover Design by Sinem Erkas
Cover Illustrations by Frieda Ruh

Acknowledgements
DK would like to acknowledge the work that has gone into the coordination and creation of this book. The book has been a collective effort with contributors around the world going above and beyond. We'd like to thank Nick Gentry for assisting Sinem Erkas with design work; Laiza Montezano for assisting Ana Strumpf; Samantha Richiardi and Sandra Perry for design support; Amy Pimperton and Dr Andrew Brooks for fact-checking; Lisa Davis and Rica Dearman for proofreading; Martin Copeland, Virien Chopra, Ridhima Sikka, Manpreet Kaur, and Ruchi Bansal for picture research. We'd also like to thank Room to Read and the team at Rebel Girls.

First published in Great Britain in 2026 by
Dorling Kindersley Limited
20 Vauxhall Bridge Road,
London SW1V 2SA

Rebel Girls and Good Night Stories for Rebel Girls are registered trademarks.
Rebel Girls is a global, multi-platform empowerment brand dedicated to helping raise the most inspired and confident generation of girls.
www.rebelgirls.com

Published by Dorling Kindersley Ltd in association with Room to Read
Room to Read is a non-profit 501(c)(3) organization and registered UK charity

The authorised representative in the EEA is
Dorling Kindersley Verlag GmbH. Arnulfstr. 124, 80636 Munich, Germany

Text and page design copyright © 2026 Dorling Kindersley Limited
A Penguin Random House Company

10 9 8 7 6 5 4 3 2 1
001–341637–Mar/2026

All rights reserved.
No part of this publication may be reproduced, stored in or introduced into a retrieval system, or transmitted, in any form, or by any means (electronic, mechanical, photocopying, recording, or otherwise), without the prior written permission of the copyright owner.
DK values and supports copyright. Thank you for respecting intellectual property laws by not reproducing, scanning, or distributing any part of this publication by any means without permission. By purchasing an authorised edition, you are supporting writers and artists and enabling DK to continue to publish books that inform and inspire readers. No part of this publication may be used or reproduced in any manner for the purpose of training artificial intelligence technologies or systems. In accordance with Article 4(3) of the DSM Directive 2019/790, DK expressly reserves this work from the text and data mining exception.

A CIP catalogue record for this book
is available from the British Library.
ISBN: 978-0-2416-8126-8

Printed and bound in Slovakia

www.dk.com

MIX
Paper | Supporting responsible forestry
FSC™ C018179

This book was made with Forest Stewardship Council™ certified paper – one small step in DK's commitment to a sustainable future.
Learn more at www.dk.com/uk/information/sustainability